Y0-BVZ-777

The Corporate Prince

Qass Aquarius

The Corporate Prince

A HANDBOOK OF ADMINISTRATIVE TACTICS

VNR
VAN NOSTRAND REINHOLD COMPANY
New York Cincinnati Toronto London Melbourne

Van Nostrand Reinhold Company Regional Offices:
New York Cincinnati Chicago Millbrae Dallas

Van Nostrand Reinhold Company International Offices:
London Toronto Melbourne

Library of Congress Catalog Card Number: 70-166402

Manufactured in the United States of America

Published by Van Nostrand Reinhold Company
450 West 33rd Street, New York, N.Y. 10001

Published simultaneously in Canada by
Van Nostrand Reinhold Ltd.

15 14 13 12 11 10 9 8 7 6 5 4 3 2 1

Foreword

When I first got into business, I met a man whom I shall call Gregory. Gregory was riding high in those days. He was vice president and creative director of a large $100 million advertising agency and the only threat to his empire was Ed, a young copy supervisor, who was one of his trusted lieutenants.

Young Ed was good. Very good. He played the game beautifully. Lunch every two weeks with Gregory's boss, Mr. Powell, the beautiful agency president. Ed would never criticize his boss, Gregory, outright. Ed would simply say, "Good old Greg. You can't beat him from keeping the troops' morale up. At 5:00 P.M. anybody from the cleaning lady on up is pulled into his office for a drink."

To this Mr. Powell, the beautiful agency president, would smile like a Cheshire cat and make a mental note. "So young Ed is telling me that Gregory is drinking too much." Sometimes, Ed would address the agency's creative review board and say things like, "I want you to know that the new creative concept for Frizzbee toothpaste is Gregory's and Gregory's alone. The man is a genius. Last week as he was running out to catch the 5:45 to Connecticut, he yelled to me over his shoulder, 'Let's say Frizzbee toothpaste contains a new tooth whitening ingredient called Pakistan. Okay, Ed, now you get some monkeys to execute it.' And without breaking his stride, Gregory was out the door. What a genius."

Of course, the creative review board sitting there listening to Ed didn't think too much of Pakistan as a miracle ingredient or Gregory for thinking about it. And when Mr. Powell, the beautiful agency president, heard Ed's little speech he thought, "So, Gregory isn't paying much attention to his job these days and he's relying on good old Ed to make excuses for him."

Soon everybody at the agency felt that it was a matter of days if not hours until Ed would get Gregory's job. They also wondered how Gregory can be so trusting and so stupid. He was letting Ed love him to death. And then one day it happened.

One Monday morning on each employee's desk there was a simple four line memo which said, "It is with a great deal of regret that I must announce the resignation of Ed ———. Ed has been a trusted and valued co-worker for the past five years and I'm sure we all wish him well on any future endeavors." The memo was signed Gregory ———.

What a switch. Young Ed had been fired. It all had come to a boil the previous Friday when young Ed felt he was strong enough to make his move for the top job. He privately met and lined up on his side every member of the creative review board. Then he made the decision. Mr. Powell, the beautiful agency president, was going to be on his side. And so he would talk to him first thing Monday morning and explain to him why he, Ed, should be the new creative director. Unfortunately, what happened was somebody squealed. Somebody told Gregory that on Monday morning he was going to get fired. Gregory simply picked up the phone and called Charlie, the president of Crashem Cars, the agency's largest account.

And so on Saturday, Mr. Powell, the beautiful agency president, found himself playing golf with Gregory, his creative director and Charlie, his client. As Charlie was teeing off on the 16th hole, Gregory leaned over and whispered to Mr. Powell, "I think I am going to have to let young Ed go. He is a troublemaker who might say something and lose the agency my good, good, good friend Charlie's Crashem Cars account." "Sh, sh, sh," said Mr. Powell, "he'll hear you." "I'll fire him tomorrow," said Gregory. "I'll call him when he gets home from church."

One day, years later, when we were both enjoying a three martini, two bottle of wine lunch, I asked Gregory about young Ed. "Jerry," he said, "young Ed really thought he was a Machiavellian character. If he had worked it so that I was fired that Friday instead of letting the weekend go by, he would be creative director today. But the schmuck probably only read half of Machiavelli's 'The Prince'. It's a cinch he never read page 97." "Page 97?" I said. "What does it say?" With this, Greg took a long satisfied puff on a cigar, leaned back, smiled and said, "It says 'never wound a king.' "

Is The Corporate Prince an honest account of what goes on in the business world? Yes, definitely yes. Will most businessmen admit this? No, definitely no. And yet I submit that there isn't a single man who has reached the top in business who hasn't at one time or another lived the life, every page, every chapter, every thought, of The Corporate Prince.

I showed the manuscript of this book to a friend of mine who is known as the most gentle, most respected man in his business. "Bullshit," he roared. "Pure bullshit. I don't believe a word of it." "Jack," I said, "why don't you sit back and think for one second about how you got to the top when so many of your friends failed." He thought for a minute and then said, "Son of a bitch, I'm so good at it that I don't even tell myself I'm doing it."

Jerry Della Femina

Preface

Some sensitive souls will be needlessly disturbed by the tactics discussed in this book. They will feel that somehow it is immoral even to study the subject of administrative tactics, let alone use them. So let us get this matter of ethics out in the open right now.

First, nowhere in this book is the use of any one tactic either recommended or not recommended—each is just presented for your information. You are the sole determinant of how you will use this information.

Second, there is nothing unethical about knowledge. Knowing about sin does not a sinner make—it requires action.

Third, a tactic is neither good nor bad. Ethical questions can only be raised about how a tactic is used. Many people might claim that it is unquestionably unethical to lie but there are situations in which the truth would do the harm while the lie would do the good. Try telling a rejected job applicant that the reason for his rejection is that his intellect leaves something to be desired. Sugar coat it as you might try, it would still come out, "You're too stupid for the job!" Now what good has been done by the alleged truth? Another tactic, a more deceiving one admittedly, would not only be wiser, but kinder.

Fourth, there is no way to avoid using tactics, some

tactics. Tactics are the means by which administrators do their jobs, execute their plans. They must use them. The question is not to use or *not* to use, but one of should it be this or that? An ineffective tactic is not more moral, more ethical, than an effective one, yet that is the essence of the argument put forth by some critics of administrative tactics who seem bent on restricting administrators to the use of only ineffective tools. And that is what tactics are—the administrator's tools.

No claim is made that this compilation of administrative tactics is exhaustive, for it most certainly is not. You are encouraged to add to it your favorite administrative ploys; most executives have them. Instead, this book is intended to introduce you to tactical thinking and give you some insights into many of the more common tactics that you may encounter.

Admittedly, some of the tactics are closely related, but they are split into separate categories when the tactics differ in some significant way or intent.

This book is written under a pseudonym because I am a coward. An earlier attempt to include some of this material in a book on management was met with great hostility by reviewers who maintained, "People shouldn't be taught such things. It isn't proper to speak of these matters, even if they are true. These are things that must be learned the hard way." Nonsense! I see little virtue in learning anything the hard way if it can be learned in an easier manner. Admittedly, there are many lessons that evidently can be learned only the "hard way," yet it seems that they are assimilated more quickly if one has been properly prepared for them.

Several top executives of rather large companies read

this manuscript and encouraged me to publish it. I would like to thank them publicly for their helpful comments, but they said they would sue if I mentioned them by name. The able tactician prefers to remain unrecognized.

As usual the real work on this book was done by my able assistant, Sylvia Arnot, who said that she wouldn't sue. This is an example of the *Give Recognition Where Due* tactic, used far too seldom.

Qass Aquarius

APRIL, 1971
EXECUTIVE BEACH, CALIFORNIA

Contents

PART TWO TIMING TACTICS

PART THREE NEGOTIATING AND PERSUASIVE TACTICS

Introduction

Certain managerial terms such as objectives, goals, strategies, tactics and policies have been used so frequently by so many different writers that is understandable that confusion exists about them. In particular, the terms "strategies" and "tactics" are frequently misunderstood. A strategy is a plan of action an administrator develops to achieve some goal, which can be either personal or organizational.

Tactics are the *behavioral maneuverings* an administrator undertakes to carry out his strategies. In military parlance, tactics are the maneuvering of men and machines to carry out a plan. A general may develop a strategy for winning a battle and then have his staff develop appropriate tactics to execute it. Indeed, a war itself may be but a tactic in some overall political strategy. Tactics are used at all levels; they are simply behavior designed to carry out a plan of action.

IMPORTANCE OF TACTICS

It is a sorrowful thing to admit, but many fine strategies with highly desirable goals have failed for want of proper tactics. A sales manager formulated a new compensation plan designed to increase both sales and the men's earnings—worthy goals. But he gave no thought to tactics; he tried a direct frontal attack, but was soundly defeated by the men who were afraid of his new plan. Other tactics could have carried the day.

Indeed, many ill-advised strategies have been effected successfully through the use of excellent tactics. One college administrator had developed an organizational plan he wished to have adopted. Unfortunately, it was a very bad plan, as subsequent events made painfully obvious. However, through adept tactical moves he overcame the opposition that could have easily sidetracked his plan under more normal circumstances. And so it may be that the successful execution of plans depends more on the tactics employed than upon their intrinsic soundness, a most lamentable circumstance. Therefore, it behooves the developer of sound plans to become tactically adept so that his plans can compete successfully with inferior competitors. Many talented young executives are thwarted in their ambitions because they operate under the naive assumption that right is might. Unfortunately, they are frequently done in by men of lesser talents who are more adept tactically. It is insufficient to devise wise strategies if they are not implemented with the proper tactics.

Unfortunately it is difficult to find much written about administrative tactics, and the reason is rather apparent. People do not like to speak or think of tactics, for it is not acceptable in our society to appear as if one is manipulating people and most tactics focus on manipulating people or structuring situations. Moreover, many tactics, when improperly applied, are considered unethical by many people. In fact, there are probably administrators who would be more willing to talk about their private lives than they would be to talk about the tactics they use in reaching their goals, and for good reason. It is usually best that other people remain unaware of the tactics being used on them.

This leaves the learning of administrative tactics up to the individual; he must learn on his own about them. This is one reason that the development of administrators is a relatively slow affair.

PROPER USE OF TACTICS

Tactics themselves are amoral—they are neither good nor bad. They are simply behavior—human behavior.

Whether or not a given tactic is correct or not in a situation depends upon many factors. There are no perfect tactics, and in a given situation there is no one *best* tactic which can be used. Many tactics may work, some better than others; many others may fail, some more surely than others.

The tactics one selects should depend upon his own personality, the personalities of the other people involved in the action, the importance of the situation, the urgency of the matter, the relationships of the parties involved and their relative powers, and other unclassifiable random factors that always exist in administrative situations. This mixture of administrator's personality with the environment and the personalities of the other parties provides the challenge in the selection of tactics. The administrator must correctly size up the situation to tailor his tactics to fit it.

All too many administrators mistakenly use the same tactics repeatedly, regardless of the circumstances. Such habits develop because those favored tactics have worked for them previously. Success reinforces the habit of using a tactic. But success can be addicting, much like the quarterback who develops a habit of throwing to a certain receiver in critical situations. There comes a time when it won't work, and that time is usually a most critical one. The adept administrator has command of a wide variety of tactics.

The classic tragedy of administrative inability to vary tactics is provided by the forceful, hard-hitting executive who, through the use of strong, authoritarian tactics, successfully climbs through the ranks, only to discover that at the top such tactics are not usually effective in dealing with others of equal ability or bent; new tactics are needed for his new environment. However, he is unable to make the necessary tactical adjustments thereby causing his failure.

Tactics are the tools of the administrator, tools he uses to effect his plans, get his way. They are much like a hammer that can be used either to pound nails or to smash thumbs. In themselves, the tools are neither good nor bad; one simply has to learn how to use them properly if he is to build houses rather than smash thumbs.

TERMINOLOGY OF PRESENTATION

For the sake of clearly identifying the parties in a tactical situation, the terms "manager, administrator, executive," or "you" will be used to designate the initiating party. Opponents are referred to as "adversaries" even though they usually are not truly adversaries in the usual sense of the word; they are not necessarily enemies. But they are the targets of the tactical undertaking and so are adversaries in one sense. This has its unfortunate connotative consequences, for it gives the impression that the administrator is constantly battling with enemies who are out to do him in. Don't be disturbed by the emotional content of the terminology. Most tactics are executed in friendly circumstances on adversaries who are unaware of being targets.

For the sake of organization, the discussion of tactics has been classified into three categories: (1) operating tactics, (2) timing tactics, and (3) negotiating and persuasive tactics. Admittedly, some of the tactics could be placed in more than one category, but that is a minor matter. Let it not bother you.

A FINAL WORD ON KEEPING YOUR PERSPECTIVE

Because of the encyclopedic nature of this book one is apt to fall into the trap of assuming that the administrator spends all his time selecting weapons from his arsenal of tactics. Nothing could be further from the truth. Such a scheming administrator would be a most miserable creature, not long for his job. In the vast majority of actions, the able administrator uses the *Honest and Straight Forward* tactic; he deals with his people and adversaries honestly and says what he means. But there are situations in which this tactic may do our hero substantial harm. It is in such circumstances that he must have ready other, more suitable, more effective tactics for his use. And so let us get on with it!

The Corporate Prince

I

OPERATING TACTICS

Operating tactics comprise the bulk of the day-to-day tactics an administrator uses in executing his daily role. In military terms, these would be called battle tactics. Keep in mind that the basic operating tactic employed by most good administrators in daily encounters is the *Honest and Straight Forward* tactic in which he tells the others the truth in a straightforward way. He says what he thinks. No cunning ploys. No devious evasions. All open and above board.

Of course, there are dangers in using this tactic as related by one college graduate who complained to his former "Human Relations" professor, "You told us to go forth and be honest and straightforward. I went forth and was honest and straightforward. I got killed. Slaughtered! I was considered a naive oaf unworthy of further advancement. You left something out of your lessons. You forgot to tell me about all those people who are not honest and who are not straightforward." Let us not go into the fray unprepared, unarmed for what we most certainly will encounter.

WHICH ROAD TO TRAVEL

There are different avenues of approach in instituting a plan of action; the administrator can select any one or a combination of several approaches—roads to follow. The wise administrator gives considerable thought to *which road to travel* for inevitably they vary in difficulty and destination. Naturally, the administrator seeks the path of least resistance and this incorporates evaluating the acceptability of his plan to various people. How much assistance and support can he pick up along each route?

A merchant constructing a store in a large mall-type regional shopping center was shocked when he learned of the mechanical specifications developed by the mechanical engineers designated by the center's management for his store area and for which he was expected to pay. They grossly overspecified 22 tons of air conditioning and far more heating capacity than was needed: cost, $14,000.

The merchant had several avenues open to him. He could protest to the shopping center's management. He could protest directly to the mechanical engineer. He could take the matter up with the proposed subcontractor who wanted the store's electrical as well as mechanical contract which were to be let by the merchant.

The merchant concluded that it would be hopeless to take issue with the mechanical engineer, for his ego was involved with the design and he would not be likely to amend his recommendations if challenged. He had developed these excessive specifications because it wasn't his client's money that was being spent and he would be professionally safe with such an overly adequate heating and air conditioning system. Similarly, the merchant decided that it would do little good to take the matter up with the management of the shopping center, for it was in their interest that such a heating and air conditioning system be installed; they would support the mechanical engineer who designed it. But the contractor who wanted the job was a different matter. The proposed mechanical and electrical subcontractor was a large firm that carried a great deal of influence with the technical management of the shopping center.

The merchant approached the owner of the contracting firm with independent estimates that only 5 tons of air conditioning capacity were needed and practically no heating. The subcontractor said that he would handle the matter with the shopping center management. The final system cost $8000.

This is an example of an assessment of *which road to follow* in executing a plan of action. Frequently the success or failure in achieving a result depends more on how one goes about it than the nature of the goal. The administrator must find a plan by which he can pick up sufficient bargaining power that he can have his way. In this case, the subcontractor had sufficient influence and power with the key decision maker that he could carry the day. The merchant in the above instance did have some direct bargaining power, if it had come down to an outright battle, for there was nothing in his lease that required him to air condition his store at all. He could have sucked enough cool air from the air conditioned mall to cool his premises but this was an ultimate tactic which did not have to be used, since the parties involved tacitly knew this without having it pointed out to them.

Sometimes the road to follow can be very round-about and devious; the direct route may not be the best. A man wants a job with a certain company. To apply directly to that company might be a mistake in many instances. Success might be more likely if he has a mutual friend place his name in the pot for the position. Indeed, many situations occur where one can go about achieving his goals only by indirect means.

THE *FAIT ACCOMPLI*—THE ACCOMPLISHED FACT

The *fait accompli* is an age-old tactic in which the administrator simply proceeds to do whatever it is that he wants to do thereby presenting his adversary with the accomplished fact rather than risking the chance of his disapproval of the plan. If the administrator is able to execute it successfully, the tactic is most effective, for there is usually little argument with success no matter if the action was outside of policy or somewhat irregular.

Be warned that the tactic does have its dangers; some superiors tend to dislike brash subordinates who seize the reins to proceed with some unauthorized venture, particularly if it is a significant affair. This tactic is the stuff from which disciplinary actions are made.

But the tactic can be most effective in dealing with people who are lethargic, indecisive, or overly conservative. Knowing the problems that await him if he should request permission for something or other, the strong administrator may decide to go ahead with it and rely on his results and overall strength in the organization to protect him. Indifference frequently allows the *fait accompli* to go unchallenged if not unnoticed. People with little or no feelings about the matter just don't take the trouble to counter the action.

If the administrator is called to explain his actions, he can frequently cover himself by playing innocent. "Gee, I didn't realize that this was something you wanted to be bothered with, boss. I'm sorry! Thought I had authority to go ahead with it, that it was the thing to do." Flash a look of innocence and there is little the boss can do about it, particularly if the result was successful. The boss who becomes upset with subordinates who successfully execute a plan without his approval is apt to appear to others as a weak, insecure administrator who lacks control of his operation, and he doesn't want that image.

The tactic works best in relatively minor matters. Don't ask your in-laws where they want to eat; they'll never agree and you'll be driving down the road for hours. Just pull in where you want to eat and present them with a *fait accompli.* Bosses favor subordinates who know when and how to use the tactic on matters they consider too trivial for their attention—"Don't bother me with it! Do it!"

Dangers are posed on more major matters, but that's where the real rewards reside. Jobs are placed on the line as some executives gamble their future on the outcome of a bold play. But then it may not be such a gamble at that if they are not particularly interested in their jobs if they are not allowed their play.

One newly hired sales manager, after interviewing each

of his twenty two salesmen, decided that fourteen of them had to go; there was no way they could ever work for him. Although the situation verged on bankruptcy, he had accepted the job because he thought he saw a way to save the day while making himself some real money. He knew that his boss would be most reluctant to fire fourteen men at once—it would scare him to death. So the *fait accompli.* He fired the fourteen men, replaced them immediately with his kind of people, and had results to show for the action before the boss could react. He had little to lose. If he couldn't flush the deadwood, he didn't want the job, as success was most doubtful. And a sales manager might reasonably expect that it was within his scope of authority to hire and fire his men.

Reasonableness is the key defense for the *fait accompli.* Make the action seem to be a reasonable one, one within your authority, and act surprised if anyone should question your right to undertake the action. Most job descriptions are so vague that the accuser seldom has solid grounds on which to stand, so the *fait accompli* feeds on the organizational confusion over who has the right to do what to whom.

SANDBAGGING

The fine art of sandbagging has been developed in the game of golf and poker, and can be applied equally to administration. The sandbagger in a poker game is the man who checks a bet and then bumps the person who does bet, thereby increasing the size of the pot over what it would have been, had he opened the bet himself. The sandbagger in golf is the hustler who has a much higher handicap than his skill warrants. He has learned the delicate art of caring for and feeding one's handicap.

The sandbagging administrator is similarly deceptive. He has mastered the art of seeming harmless and without power, but in reality he carries far more authority and clout than one would be led to believe. Sometimes his power is sub rosa, not easily detected except by those who have observed the scene for some period of time. Other administrators sandbag by their seemingly pleasant, disarming personality; they seem friendly and harmless but, in reality, are anything but.

The sandbagging administrator sometimes will apparently go along with some plan of action, but secretly he is against it. He does this merely to lull the adversary into a sense of security and well-being; the administrator has every intention of sandbagging the plan in some manner or another at a later date. Sometimes the administrator actually gives his consent to some plan proposed by an adversary with the full intention of sandbagging it in some way later.

This tactic is used when, for reasons of organizational politics, it would not be wise to openly oppose the plan.

A rather pedestrian department head disapproved of a program proposed by one of his men, but he felt that he could not openly veto it for fear that it would not only solidify opposition to his leadership but would look bad to his superior. So he seemingly encouraged the subordinate in his endeavor but killed the program at budget time by failing to find funds for it. "Sorry, Charley! Just couldn't get the money for you." And the *sandbag* claimed another victim.

CHOOSE YOUR BATTLEGROUND

The actual scene or environment in which contact with an adversary takes place is not something which may be left to chance, but should be considered very carefully. It may be wise to see some men in social environments rather than in the office. Frequently men are more relaxed and more congenial in a social setting, particularly under pleasant, relaxing circumstances, than they are in a business environment. Sometimes the administrator should create the proper scene. In other words, the administrator can create his own battleground, one that he feels will facilitate whatever plan he has in mind.

In a business context, consideration should be given to the question of whose office or where contacts should be made: his office or yours or someone else's.

Sometimes a superior can gain advantages by intimidating subordinates through contact in the superior's office, but this is not always so. Sometimes subordinates can be impressed if the superior comes to their office, particularly if it looks like a casual visit. Sometimes executives have special rooms or comfortable lounges for creating a permissive atmosphere in which to relax.

Sometimes an adversary can be placed in a situation in which he cannot oppose your plan because of the witnesses who are present.

Fundamentally, the selection of a battle ground comes down to determining the influence that the administrator wants the atmosphere to have on the adversary. Does he want the environment to intimidate or influence the target, or does he want the environment to relax and lower the adversary's guard? A personnel manager for a large corporation was instituting a plan whose goal was to procure more and better college graduates for his firm. In particular, he wished to influence a certain professor to guide him to outstanding graduates. He wisely decided that his country club would be the best environment in which to gain the professor's cooperation. Armstrong Cork pursued a similar plan on a nation-wide scale for several years. It invited a large number of professors to various central locations for a one day program at the company's expense; it created a permissive environment in which it could present its plan.

BE PRESENT ON THE BATTLEFIELD

There are times when an administrator executes a plan through subordinates, much as a general fights a war through his chain of command. Nevertheless, most good generals attempt to stay close to the battlefield for many reasons: communications are quicker and more accurate; more flexibility can be inserted into plans, should they need revision due to the course of events; and the presence of the administrator at the battlefield can have a positive effect on one's forces and a negative one on the opposition.

The administrator should be present when one of his subordinates is presenting a plan which he particularly desires to be successful; he should lend his support and the authority of his position to his subordinate lest he expose his subordinate to counter-attacks which may shoot down the plan in such a way that it would be difficult to revive it later. Once a plan has been defeated, it will stiffen the backbone of the opposition; they can always claim that the matter has been settled previously and, therefore, should not be brought up again.

Naturally, there are instances when the administrator should be absent from the battlefield: when he knows things are going to be brought up and said that he does not want to hear, he should vanish. Sometimes one's subordinates can say things that the administrator cannot say, or would not care to be on record as having said.

A more pressing engagement prevented a dean from attending a routine faculty meeting. Suddenly the dean's supporters had their hands full trying to table several outrageous motions put forth by the dean's adversaries who had decided to take advantage of his absence to trim his authority. When the cat's away . . .

MAKE CERTAIN PREPARATIONS ARE COMPLETE BEFORE BATTLE

One should go into battle fully armed. Some administrators are undone by their carelessness; before going into battle they fail to make certain that they are properly prepared, to their eventual undoing.

An executive was going before his board of directors with a proposal for the marketing plan for a new product. His preparation had been rather half-baked. There were several salient questions that he had left unanswered. After his formal presentation, several sharp-minded directors quickly made a shambles of his presentation with questions in areas he had slighted. He looked like a fool and his career was destroyed in that company. He resigned shortly after the incident, when advancement appeared improbable.

TOUCH ALL BASES

Frequently it is critical to attend to all the details involved in a situation. Touch all bases—to insure that no strings are left untied. Sometimes this means doing the paperwork, while at other times it means seeing all the people involved. One base left untouched may be the undoing of a plan. This is particularly true in attending to legal matters. The wise administrator makes certain to touch all the legal bases concerning his operation, attending to all the little details such as proper minutes of stockholder and board meetings, and executing all the legal niceties that are sometimes so seemingly useless until trouble arises.

The president and majority stockholder of a corporation ran it as his own domain with no attention to legal aspects of corporation law, such as holding formal stockholder meetings, board meetings, keeping proper minutes, etc. He reasoned that he and the other two stockholders were so close that nothing would happen and there was no need for such nonsense. All was fine until two of them fell out with the third, at which time the third was able to use all of the untouched bases as trump cards in negotiating the settlement.

PERSONALIZE

Men seem to like to associate best with others who seem personable. Cold fish are disdained. The administrator who is always overly businesslike will seldom engender warm feelings toward him from others. A great many things are done by subordinates for their superiors solely for personal reasons. The secretary who stays after hours to get out needed letters, the production workers who work extra time to get out a particular order, and many other such examples that happen daily are the result of personal feelings, personal relationships between worker and boss. Such relationships are difficult to establish at best; they are impossible unless the administrator has learned to personalize his approach to his people.

Take the matter of names. How can a worker think that his boss really recognizes him and his work if he continually refers to him as "You over there!" Use names, first names when appropriate. Write little personal notes to people when the occasion warrants; drop by their office to make the appropriate remarks when they have an addition to the family or other personal event which should not go unnoticed. One administrator made a big thing of birthdays. He reasoned that this was the only ritualistic event that was truly personal with the individual, so he made certain that his subordinates' birthdays did not go unnoticed.

On a larger scale, significant business decisions can be influenced by personal appeals. The top executive of one small contract manufacturing concern operated on a personal basis in getting most of his business. By a well formulated, thoughtful program of socializing and entertainment, he developed close relationships with most of the key personnel in the companies from which he wanted business. It is easy to turn down bids from men you don't know; it is a far different matter when you know them well.

Sometimes a direct appeal for a personal favor will win the day when appeals to logic have failed. "I would appreciate it if you would do this as a favor to me." Implicit in this statement is that you will in turn do him a favor when the occasion arises, so don't be surprised to find the bill collector at your door at some future time.

HOLD YOUR COAT

At times the administrator wants no part of a battle. There are situations in which one is bound to be burned if he gets into the fray, so he should stay on the sidelines and watch the play, rather than acquiring bruises in it. However, the administrator may have a stake one way or the other in the affair, so he uses the *hold your coat* tactic, in which he provides support to the warrior of his choice by doing everything possible short of going into battle with him. This is a particularly wise decision if one believes that the warrior may go down to defeat and one does not wish to go down with him.

Sometimes *hold your coat* is used to encourage someone to do battle, knowing that he will be destroyed, to the ultimate advantage of the administrator.

An executive with a large consumer goods company was rather controversial in the organization because of his aggressive personality. On one occasion, he stormed into an associate's office with the notice of his annual wage increase—$1000. He asked, "How much of a raise did you get?"

The associate truthfully replied, "$2000." This added fuel to the man's fire; he threatened to do all sorts of things, including walking into the boss' office, slamming down the notice of the pay increase, and resigning. The associate commiserated with him and agreed that he had certainly been mistreated, that something should be done about the humiliation.

Actually, the associate had no objection at all to the man's resigning, for if he did the associate would gain certain advantages and additional strengths in the organization. So he executed *hold your coat.* The man did resign and the associate gained an additional raise for having to take over a few additional duties, which were no particular problem to him.

Sometimes *hold your coat* is used to soften up adversaries. The administrator encourages a number of other people to battle with the adversary prior to his engagement with him, in the hope that the adversary will be softened up by the continual onslaught and tire of fighting. In one company, a man did nothing to discourage four other men from resigning for various reasons when they came to him to talk about their plights. He would offer no hope for them, thereby encouraging them to quit. After the four men had resigned within the month, he went in to quit, too. He was able to extract most of what he wanted from his superior, who was now in a panic over what seemed to him to be a mass resignation of his entire group. It is indeed a wise administrator who learns how to use others to fight his battles for him, or to soften up adversaries in anticipation of battles to come.

This is a relatively safe tactic to use, if done with discretion. The administrator avoids the line of fire and need not take a strong position or say or do things to incur the wrath of the victors-to-be. It should almost always be used when one's allies are going up against very powerful adversaries—ones who are almost inevitably going to be the victors. There is little use in deliberately getting involved in a battle which is doomed from the start.

FRONTAL ATTACK

There are certainly times when the administrator should walk right up to the adversary and make a *frontal attack.* This tactic is best used when the administrator knows that he is completely right and he is dealing from a position of overwhelming strength. Under such circumstances there may be nothing to lose and quite a bit to gain by making a *frontal attack* that may even be quite obvious to all around. There are instances in which if one does not make a *frontal attack,* other people will be disappointed with him and lose confidence in his ability to make forthright decisions and act on them. One salesman clearly violated company policy by moonlighting on the side after he had been warned not to do so. His sales manager directly confronted him with the evidence and dismissed him on the spot when the moonlighting salesman admitted his errant behavior.

The *frontal attack* probably should be used by a good administrator far more often than it is. After all, it is the cheapest and most direct route to the desired goal, and if it is handled correctly, the results should be quite satisfactory.

Unfortunately, some people have personalities which almost preclude the use of a *frontal attack* on them; they seem to automatically bow their backs and get ready for a fight anytime someone comes at them directly. There are obstinate, stubborn, contrary people. A *frontal attack* with such individuals not only is a waste of time but actually may serve notice on them which may allow them to defeat the plan.

Frontal attack is not advisable when one is in a weak position. If the administrator is a voice in the wilderness, then he will have to use more guile to carry the day; the *frontal attack* will result in nothing but bruises to his ego.

THE STEAM ROLLER—THE POWER PLAY

Sheer weight of numbers can carry the day against weaker opponents if one cares not about the feelings of the other parties. Or force of feelings may be a workable substitute for use against those who hold their opinions lightly; a sufficiently strong show of feeling on your part may win out against a number of people not so highly motivated.

A branch operation was badly divided into two power groups—the in's and the out's—with the in's having control and numbers. Although for a while the in's tried to cooperate and work closely with the out's not wanting to push the separation any further, it soon became apparent to all the in's that there was no placating the adversaries. Everything the in's were in favor of, the out's were against automatically. They obstructed in every manner conceivable. Finally, the administrator resorted to the power play—we do it our way or you get out. And he had the muscle to back up his decisions. He only had to use authority once and the out's got the message.

While few people like to resort to the power play, still there comes a time when that is the only thing the adversary respects. If so, the administrator who is reluctant to use his power will suffer.

OUTFLANK 'EM!

The classic battlefield tactic for overcoming an adversary is to go around him—flank 'em. This tactic is also highly useful in business. Instead of meeting an adversary head on, the administrator simply goes around him in some manner, thereby avoiding a fight.

A young man in a large corporation was having his career jeopardized by a superior who was holding him back. The young man outflanked the superior by requesting a transfer to another division for ostensibly good and valid reasons, and was able to continue his climb up the corporate ladder under more favorable superiors.

There are certain dangers involved in trying to outflank some particularly powerful adversary who doesn't care to be outflanked and who would move to block it. A direct confrontation may result. The administrator must make certain that the person who is being outflanked will be unable to do anything about it.

THROW YOUR OWN PARTY

An interesting associate once espoused and practiced a rather effective counter tactic; should he not be invited to some party he felt that he should have been invited to, he would quickly throw one of his own, and go out of his way to make his party more attractive than its competitor. Moreover, he would try to steal some of the key guests programed for the other affair. "If they don't want you at their party, throw one of your own."

This tactic can work equally well in business, although admittedly it can appear to be rather petty at times. The president of a large downtown department store was snubbed rather badly and deliberately by the leadership of a certain charity drive. So he organized a non-profit charitable foundation of his own to which he devoted his attention. While to many people this example no doubt seems silly, and I must confess that it fails to strike me favorably, still I will admit that there are times when it is important to an administrator's position, his image with the people with whom he does business, that he not allow another person to "put him down." It is a matter of prestige, power. And these things are not to be taken lightly.

It would have been a cleverer executive who would have found another way "to Throw His Own Party," one not so obviously done out of pique, for he risked being considered childish.

ONE-ON-ONE

Sometimes an administrator endeavors to go *one-on-one* with adversaries; that is, he singles them out individually rather than facing them in groups. He wants a two-way dialogue with no other parties involved.

One-on-one should be considered when you face a situation in which there are several people involved in a matter and you feel that they may oppose what you want to do. You want a chance to persuade each individually without their reinforcing each other's opinions. People are more receptive to an idea if they are unaware of opposition to it than if they learn that other people also disagree with it. By using *one-on-one* the administrator attempts to block off the reinforcing actions of the opposition. This is particularly wise where the administrator could be overwhelmed easily by the sheer weight of numbers, no matter how right he may be. He might be perfectly correct in wanting to do a certain thing, but if all his subordinates were to oppose him, he might find it difficult to undertake the action.

Moreover, some administrators are particularly adept at dealing with one person but lose effectiveness when dealing with more at the same time. For those managers who are at their best in dealing man-to-man rather than man-to-group, the wisdom of using *one-on-one* is obvious.

A newly hired sales manager for a firm that was floundering on the verge of bankruptcy quickly perceived that some rather drastic changes had to be made in salesforce management policies. Among his more controversial plans was the changing of the company's method of paying its salesmen, who had been receiving compensation vastly disportionate to their true value to the firm. While his superior suggested that all the salesmen be called to a meeting at which the new operating policies and compensation plan would be explained to them as a group, the sales manager chose to use the *one-on-one* tactic by visiting each salesman in his territory to sell him on the entire program, including accepting lower earnings in some cases. If he had called all 35 salesmen together to break the news to them, the meeting could have easily snowballed into a mass protest with each salesman becoming increasingly indignant at management; the meeting could have degenerated into chaos. By isolating each man—*one-on-one*—the manager had the opportunity to sell his program, give the reasons for changes. Not being exposed to the emotional stimuli which would have been forthcoming at a meeting, most men were rational about the proposed plan. The objections of the few men who aggressively opposed the plan were thereby contained and not allowed to excite the other men.

In another instance *one-on-one* was used to sound out the opposition on a proposed organizational change. A young woman, who had assumed responsibility for supervising a secretarial pool of fifteen typists, saw a need for several changes in procedures to improve the work flow and relationships between the secretarial pool and the various executives using it. She developed a plan to remedy the observed defects. Although she was certain that there would be some opposition to her plan of action, she was uncertain from whom it would come. She used the *one-on-one* tactic in sounding out each of the administrators being served by the secretarial pool to see if he had any objections to her plan and, if so, what they were and how they could be met. After sounding out the executives, she discovered that, with a few minor revisions, her plan was acceptable. She issued a memorandum which stated, "In accordance with my recent conversation with you regarding the work flow in the secretarial pool and the excellent suggestions you made, the following procedures will be . . ."

The *one-on-one* tactic may backfire if the various people contacted are able to get together quickly to compare notes and discover that, as a group, they have strong feelings against the administrator's plan. The tactic works best if the adversaries are physically so situated that it is difficult for them to get together, or if they are not likely to compare notes because of their positions or social groupings

Unless the administrator deliberately wants to play one man against another, he should take great care not to give that appearance by telling different stories which, upon comparison, would quickly disclose his game. The administrator's game may be destroyed once the opposition discovers he is playing one against another and they unite to put down his gambit. In the *one-on-one* tactic the administrator is not trying to divide the men at all. He wants them to remain an effective, operating, cooperative unit.

DIVIDE AND CONQUER

Although *divide and conquer* appears to be closely akin to *one-on-one*, they are really two different tactics. In *divide and conquer,* the administrator may not be dealing with individuals *one-on-one,* but instead may be trying to divide two or more interest groups. Sometimes *divide and conquer* will also use *one-on-one* tactics.

Divide and conquer evolves in a situation in which the opposition is composed of several interest groups who have formed a coalition against a plan and have put aside their differences to organize against a common enemy.

In recent years *divide and conquer* has been the basic tactic of Soviet Russia in opposing NATO. It has continually tried to insert wedges between each of the member nations of NATO, playing on their jealousies and special interests in prying them away from the common group, the NATO Alliance. We can see that in the field of politics *divide and conquer* is a widely used tactic, but how about its use in business administration?

Make no mistake, in some situations it can be a dangerous tactic to use, particularly when you must get along with the opposition on a continuing basis after the impending administrative action. The administrator employing *divide and conquer* tactics risks being considered Machiavellian, but this need not stay his hand, for there are certainly times when it is the correct tactic to employ.

To apply *divide and conquer,* keep each adversary aware of his differences with the other groups, keep stressing that your interests and his have much more in common. Your major message is that it is more to his interest to ally himself with you than with the other adversaries; at least you hope to neutralize him in the matter.

An executive vice president of a manufacturing concern found himself in the unenviable position of administering a group of functional vice presidents, each of whom was an aggressive empire builder in competition with the others. He managed to keep control of the operation through continual use of the *divide and conquer* tactic. He kept each of the vice presidents loyal to him by not trying to solve their jealousies, but rather using them to gain support. In many subtle ways he kept the men continually worried that their counterparts might get ahead of them in some respect or another. Each man was loyal because he thought that the executive vice president was his best friend in the organization and that he benefited from this allegiance.

Divide and conquer has even been used upward. One young assistant plant manager had a boss who was continually feuding with his peers. The boss routinely came into the assistant's office to let off steam about some injustice. The assistant took care to make the proper remarks, sympathizing with the superior's plight, adding whatever fuel he could, here and there, to keep the boss steamed up. The assistant had several ulterior motives. First, he wanted his boss' job and thought that if the man exploded in some company fight, he might get it. Second, since the boss had so many running fights within the organization, he greatly needed the assistant for psychological support. This strengthened the assistant's position, so he received good pay raises and favorable treatment because his boss badly needed him.

Divide and conquer can only be used when there is a real basis for the division. When the administrator manufactures—or attempts to take advantage of—minor differences in order to split up the opposition, it may backfire on him and he will then face a united adversary whose backbone has been stiffened by the attempted use of this tactic.

If the administrator tries to use this tactic continually for small things, it will lead to his destruction.

If the administrator does not have a continual relationship with his adversaries, he can rather openly use *divide and conquer.* Otherwise, he must use great finesse and subtlety in dividing potential adversaries, lest they become aware of what he is trying to do. It is quite possible to divide adversaries without their realizing it because of the strong emotions that are involved when someone harbors a grudge against another. Such emotions can be stimulated easily with little danger of discovery. Sometimes the adroit administrator is able to apply the necessary dividing stimuli through third parties, thereby relieving himself of the apparent blame.

MARSHAL YOUR FORCES OR TURN OUT THE GUARD

Sometimes in a controversy, the administrator finds it necessary to marshal all of his forces in preparation for a confrontation with an adversary; he sees a need to overwhelm the adversary with sheer weight of numbers.

The cost of marshaling one's forces can be high, for the administrator can only do so a limited number of times before his forces tire of the exercise. One university dean would marshal his entire faculty for critical faculty meetings in order to offset the power massed by the dean of another school, but his ability to turn out the vote at a series of these crucial faculty meetings lamed with the passing of time.

The administrator can only make an impassioned plea about the criticalness of a meeting a limited number of times, so he should be quite careful to marshal the forces only in truly critical instances.

AIM AT STRENGTH

Some administrators have successfully used the tactic of aiming at an adversary's strength, under the theory that when you defeat his strength his entire defense must collapse. Of course, an administrator using this tactic must be certain he can defeat the enemy's strength, lest he be defeated in turn.

One merchant, in locating his quality apparel shop, selected a location right next to his leading competitor and set about to whip the adversary in the very lines in which he was strongest. Through adroit merchandising, he succeeded in luring away some of the adversary's best lines and in a period of eight years managed to become four times as large as the competitor. Another apparel operator located in the same region attempted to compete by aiming at the dominant store's weaknesses, only to fail.

AIM AT WEAKNESS

A most common tactic is to spot a weakness in an adversary and take advantage of it; keep pounding at it, aim all actions at it, until the adversary falls. A football coach spots an opponent's weak defensive backfield man and that player will see footballs coming his way all afternoon. A weak defensive tackle can expect a large amount of traffic in his direction all afternoon. "Find the Achilles' heel and aim at it." Men have their weaknesses, and they have been destroyed by them. One administrator destroyed a competing fellow executive by getting him drunk at the most inopportune time during an affair where key people were present.

Weaknesses can take forms other than habits. Sometimes an executive will have certain areas of his organization that are in trouble or that are weak performers. These are areas in which he is vulnerable to criticism. Executives have been known to be neutralized in their criticism of others by the existence of their own "glass houses." They cannot throw stones at another executive for fear that he will start stoning them.

Sometimes in a discussion an adept administrator is able to keep it focused in areas in which an adversary is not expert. This is a favorite gambit of the quantitative man; he likes to talk in technical terms and stay in areas where the non-quantitative executive cannot even comprehend him, let alone counter him. It takes a brave adversary to counter this tactic, an adversary confident of his own judgment and prestige in a situation.

RUN FOR DAYLIGHT

This tactic, named for the famed maneuver by fullback Jim Taylor of the Green Bay Packers, aptly describes a tactic of an administrator who sees a hole or opportunity and pursues it with great vigor. This is a most desirable tactic. Dame Fortune smiles upon those who see opportunities and take advantage of them while the timid are left among the mass of the mediocre, too afraid to run for daylight.

There are few dangers involved in employing this tactic, except that one may fall on his face and fail to make it, but even so most people admire those who try.

A young rising publishing executive, ensconced in a relatively high executive position with a large company, was offered an opportunity to head up the publishing division of a large conglomerate. The change involved considerable risk, for there was a high probability that he would fail, but he seized the opportunity and is now running as hard as he can for daylight. It appears that he will make it. It appears that more daylight is opening up for him, as another firm has approached him to form an even larger operation in which he will be the chief operating executive.

The problem with this tactic is that all too many middle management administrators really cannot see the holes and, when they do, they are afraid to run for daylight.

SPEED

Plain, unadulterated *speed* is frequently a most successful tactic. History is replete with examples of battles won simply because one general was able to get somewhere faster than another. Business history is loaded with examples of firms that succeeded simply because they got to a market first. Executive action is no different. The president of a small manufacturing company was suddenly informed one morning by his two senior vice presidents that they intended to oust him from the company by gaining control of the proxies at the next stockholder's meeting. They told him that they had come to the conclusion that he was wasting time and that the company no longer needed him. The president immediately climbed aboard an airplane and visited a sufficient number of major stockholders of the company to gain their proxies; there were two very surprised vice presidents at the meeting when they were informed that they were out. Speed and personal contact carried the day.

An editor for a large publishing house heard via the grapevine that a certain highly desirable manuscript was being sought by three of his leading competitors, all of whom were getting reviews of it. While they were dilly-dallying around with reviews, the editor hopped on an airplane, flew out and signed the author to a contract.

Some deals go to the man who beats his adversary by only a few minutes. Tomorrow may be too late in certain transactions. In this age of the jet and the telephone there is little excuse for an executive who sits back and waits for the U.S. mail to firm up a critical deal for him.

THE TRAP PLAY

The basic thinking underlying the *trap play* is to fool the adversary into thinking he sees a weakness in your plan which he will pursue vigorously—sometimes basing his whole defense on it—only to be destroyed when you spring the trap.

One large electronics firm, in negotiating cost changes amounting to about $500,000 with the U.S. Army, based its entire claim on an extremely lengthy theoretical presentation of what it should cost the company for all of the unwarranted work stoppages that had been caused by government representatives in violation of the contract. No mention in the presentation was made of actual, realized total costs on the contract. This was originally done because the actual costs were difficult to compute and to attribute specifically to any one work stoppage by the government representatives. However, any adversary would quickly see in the voluminous report—no matter how cleverly done it might have been—that the entire case was built upon theory; the theory of the learning curve and the effect on productivity of work stoppages.

The Army contracting officer quickly seized upon this weaknesses for his major counter-attack, claiming that although this theory was fine and good, the government was not going to pay off on theory. It needed cold, hard facts. He was trapped into making a statement that the government would pay on actual costs, not theory. When asked by the company representatives, "Then it is your contention that you would only be willing to pay the actual increase in costs?" the Army officer replied, "That is correct."

In anticipation of this counter attack, the electronics company's executives had held in reserve another report showing its total actual increase in costs, which significantly exceeded the theoretical totals it was claiming. The contracting officer was trapped. He had tentatively agreed to something in the belief that he had his adversary defeated, only to be demolished by his own argument.

Many times an adversary, when he thinks that he is successfully counterattacking and gaining a great deal of ground by pursuing one line of attack, gets carried away with himself and makes extreme statements or commitments based on that counterattack. Salesmen frequently use this tactic when they employ what is known as the "trap close." The prospect makes a strong objection to something or other. The salesman, knowing full well that he can meet that objection completely, gets the prospect to commit himself that if his objection is answered, he will definitely buy the product. Sometimes he will even have the man sign a sales contract with the provision that the particular objection, perhaps it is price or delivery, be met first. Once the man is on paper, it is difficult for him to back out.

HARASS

Sometimes administrators who are in a position where they cannot win a clear cut victory over some adversary may choose to harass the foe in such a manner that he will eventually give way. Such harassments can be quite subtle and almost invisible if the administrator is sufficiently clever. Sometimes administrators use this technique to fire—to force a man to resign. Frequently it is politically unwise to outright fire a man, but he can be harassed to the point where he will resign. His budgets can be trimmed, his best men can be transferred out from under him, his privileges can be withdrawn, his authority can be reduced, he can be snubbed, by-passed, and soon he gets the message and moves on. Usually men have sufficient pride that unfair treatment and continual lowering of status will cause them to go elsewhere.

One significant minority stockholder in a closed corporation was being frozen out by the majority stockholder. Since the law really offered little assistance to him, the only tactic open to him was continual harassment through stockholder suits aimed at various malpractices of which the management was guilty, until management concluded it was best to settle with him.

Of course, harassing techniques may backfire if the adversary becomes angered and has sufficient power to counter attack or withstand the harassment. The psychological makeup of the adversary is most important in determining the eventual success of harassment. Some people simply cannot stand up under a long period of harassment, where others seem to thrive on prolonged skirmishes.

One thing should be made clear to the person being harassed: what he must do to stop the harassment. This can cause a problem, for many times it is difficult to directly approach the adversary on the subject and the proposition sounds very much like blackmail. More subtle means are necessary for getting the message to the adversary.

KEEP CLOSE

There are times, in the affairs of administrators, when it is a wise move to *keep close* to one's adversaries, thus keeping apprised of their actions. Obviously, keeping close is most advisable in situations in which rapid developments are occurring and the tide of affairs can change quickly.

One should keep constantly available to one's allies for consultation and decisions whenever the need arises. One businessman was involved in a vicious proxy fight for control of a medium size corporation. He had strong support by some able executives within the company, but he made the mistake of taking a vacation where his allies could not contact him at a most crucial time; the opposition elected their man.

GET LOST!

There comes a time when the tactic opposite of keeping close should be employed: *get lost!* Sometimes it is highly advantageous if one cannot be contacted by certain people. One young man involved in a highly explosive battle for a top coaching position was advised to leave town and get lost until supporters had secured the head coaching position for him. Unfortunately, he did not take their advice, but remained at home. An enterprising reporter got to him and the man felt compelled to answer a few questions with what he thought were the right answers. Unfortunately, these comments so angered the people in power that he immediately lost the job, which ironically had been decided in his favor only two hours before. Unquestionably, if the man had just been able to stay out of circulation until his appointment had been confirmed, he would be a head coach today at a major university, but instead today he is an assistant coach at another school.

Sometimes no matter what a man says, it will be wrong,

and to remain silent will anger still others. The brutal truth is that under such circumstances one must not see anybody if he is to keep from making a mistake. Get lost and remain incommunicado.

This tactic is usually most advisable in highly explosive situations in which all parties need to cool off and the presence of the administrator can do nothing but add fuel to some fire. President Johnson probably used this tactic quite well during the 1968 Democratic convention at which his presence would have probably done nothing but add to the chaos and confusion.

Getting lost can be an effective way of saying no without actually being forced to say it. On some timely matter on which a decision must be made, or else the whole issue will pass, a wise administrator who wishes to say no without saying it may just let the whole thing pass by without saying a thing by getting himself lost. This is closely akin to a presidential pocket veto. There are many ways of saying no without saying it.

GIVE 'EM A FLAT TIRE TO RUN ON

Ever try to go very far on a flat tire? It's rough! A newly promoted executive vice president of a medium-size manufacturing company was sent back to the banks of the Charles River to become a more skilled administrator, a more adroit businessman. He learned among other things in those hallowed halls of Ivy during his short stay in its Executive Development program that participative management was good. He learned about Theory X and Theory Y and that Y was good and X was bad. He was told he had marketing myopia, that innovation was to be the salvation of his economic soul. So he returned filled with such enthusiasm, with such purpose. Now his plant was ably managed by a man who had spent many long years with his nose to the grindstone. But no matter, Flat Nose would have to innovate, and do so by allowing his people to participate. The plant needed a committee for innovation it was decreed and Flat Nose was to appoint it.

Now Flat Nose had spent a good deal of time getting his shop to operating in just the way he wanted it to run and was not about to let this Charles River fever get loose among his crew. He appointed the committee as ordered. On it he put the two most outspoken young men in the organization but he also placed them in the company of three old mossbacks who would vote to rescind the development of the wheel. Flat tires come in many forms but the end result is the same—the vehicle goes nowhere.

The administrator can control what he wants done in an organization by the men he selects to do it. If he really wants something accomplished, then he must assign the work to a performer. If he wants to go through the motions for appearances, then he places the responsibility on someone in whom he has absolute confidence that nothing will happen.

LET THEM FURNISH THEIR OWN ROPE

Sometimes it is wise to allow the opposition to go ahead with its plans without opposing them, if one is certain that they will fail in doing so. "Give them enough rope, and let 'em hang themselves!" This tactic is particularly useful in situations in which the actions proposed by the adversaries will not be particularly harmful to the administrator and he can allow them to proceed with little or no long-run harm to his position.

Sometimes he should take care that he not furnish the rope, for he must be able to say, "I told you so," by going on record in a most polite way against the proposed action.

The administrator should be careful not to take a position in which he will be embarrassed if the opposition's plan is successful. He should not stick his neck out in opposition to them or visibly oppose or attempt to undermine their plans His hands should be clean if and when the plan fails

One young ambitious engineer for a large aircraft company had a boss who was addicted to golf; he would sneak out at every opportunity for a round, while the young man covered for him. The subordinate encouraged this behavior by being quite willing to do his superior's work. It was only a matter of time before the man's excessive absences were noted by top management and he was invited to draw his paycheck from another company. The subordinate got his job. As a matter of fact, this same young man used this tactic on three successive occasions to rise higher and higher in organizations, until he is now a vice president of a large aircraft company.

It was not golf in this instance that was the culprit, but rather the basic tactics of encouraging one's superior, *sub rosa,* to be negligent in carrying out his corporate duties until top management caught the man. Sometimes subordinates have been known to speed up this discovery indirectly by arranging to have management's attention drawn to the situation.

PUSH 'EM OFF THE DOCK

Some administrators practice the "push 'em off the dock" school of hard knocks in training their men. Give the new salesman a minimum of training, hand him an order book, point him toward the door, and shove hard. While experience indicates that this is not a good tactic to use in a good many instances, still there are times when it is the correct onc to apply to a situation. Good mcn may grow fastcst when presented with a task for which they are not completely prepared and told to swim or drown. One thing about the tactic—it separates the men from the boys.

Push 'em off the dock is best used when the man is not apt to be destroyed by the experience. One professor would use this tactic to teach his students the use of the library. He would give the class a long list of information that was to be located; he showed them where the library was located on campus and turned them loose. By the time they were through thrashing around trying to find what they needed, they had a good idea of what was in those musty stacks.

The key to using this tactic successfully lies in appraising the liklihood of the man's drowning. If he can do the job, then it can provide excellent developmental training for him.

USE A HATCHET MAN

When dirty work must be done, the wise administrator tries to keep his hands clean. Perhaps he may have a subordinate, a hatchet man, to do his dirty work for him, thereby avoiding the displeasure of those who do not approve of the actions. For this reason many administrators prefer to have their subordinates do their firing for them. Sometimes a board of directors deliberately brings in a president as a hatchet man to clean house, prune the corporate tree of its deadwood, thereby incurring great displeasure among people within the organization. After all the bloodletting has taken place, the board can find other work for the hatchet man and a new man can be brought in who immediately bestows benefits upon a greatful, relieved organization.

One college president was undone because his hatchet man refused to do the dirty work, thereby forcing the president to bloody his hands, thus incurring the wrath of the faculty and students. Normally, the dean of men is supposed to administer discipline, but this college president was unfortunate to have a dean who lacked the necessary backbone. Instead, the dean referred the cases to the president's office. While the dean of men did not last long, neither did the president who had to handle the dean's messes.

There is always dirty work to be done in any organization and any administrator who believes otherwise is naive. There are people who need to be fired, budgets that need to be cut, bad news that needs to be given, and discipline to be administered. No one likes a person who administers discipline, regardless of how correct it may be. It is amazing to watch an organization coming to the moral support of a member who has been fired, when only shortly before everyone was crying for his scalp because of his incompetency. The administrator who fires people is apt to be a villain in the eyes of the organization.

DON'T BURN YOUR BRIDGES BEHIND YOU

The age-old tactic is still as sound today as it was years ago, for generals and administrators from time immemorial have made the mistake of burning the bridges behind them that they later needed. This is probably one mistake that is made more frequently in society today than any other. In the heat of anger upon resignation or some other occurrence, an individual says or does things that permanently alienate others. He does this in the belief that these people will never be in a position in the future to affect his fortunes. Unfortunately, all too frequently these chickens come home to roost at some future time; he runs into one of the bridges he burned, and is promptly stymied. One never knows what the future holds for him or people with whom he will come in contact. Some inconsequential clerk may someday be in a position to stymie the administrator's plan. The salesman who alienates a receptionist may find that she is able to torpedo his sale to her boss.

The wise man goes even further—he goes out of his way to keep his bridges in good repair.

LEAVE THE DOOR OPEN

An administrator should try to behave toward an adversary in such a way that the door is always left open for the two to get together on their differences. Care should be taken in what is said and done that the door is not permanently closed on communications between the two and relationships between them permanently severed. For this reason, ultimatums should be avoided for they have a tendency to be final and force an adversary to do things the administrator will not appreciate. One keeps the door open by refraining from making remarks that are final, and by using such words as "perhaps, maybe, might" and avoiding definite finalizing exclamations such as, "under no circumstances . . . " Also, actions such as firing an individual or resigning can definitely slam the door.

Admittedly, there are situations in which one wants to slam the door because he wishes to push an adversary into action. Suppose an administrator wished a subordinate would resign. He might clearly tell the man that under no circumstances would he be given a raise or promotion in the future. To leave the door open might encourage the man sufficiently that he wouldn't make the desired resignation.

SURRENDER QUICKLY

At times the matter at issue of such insignificance to the administrator, or the various outcomes are a matter of relative indifference, that he is best advised to allow the adversary to win the point by quickly surrendering to his point of view. No fight, no contest. Few things will make a man quite as happy, or disarm him for future conflicts, than to win his day almost uncontested. Of course, you may wish to combine the surrender tactic with *Capitalize on Defeat* to gain some ground in other areas, but that is up to you.

There is no sense in fighting every battle with every adversary. One must be careful to conserve his ammunition and energies for the battles that matter.

And another thing: when surrendering, do so with style and poise. Don't act like a loser or begrudge the man his victory. Be forthright! If the other man is right, tell him so. Nobody likes a poor loser, so smile even though you may be bleeding inside.

RUN FOR COVER

There can be a time for tactical retreat—*run for cover*—without surrendering. Sometimes the opposition is so strong and the situation so explosive that to offer battle would be disastrous, no matter how right the administrator may be and how wrong the opposition is. Other times you may not be ready for battle and should take cover until prepared. Philosophers have written about discretion being the better part of valor and that one should run away to live and fight another day; these are reflections of the *run for cover* tactic, which the wise administrator will have use for, sooner or later. The General Motors executive who had Ralph Nader tailed would have probably been wiser to *run for cover* when discovered than to have fought it out. The Shell Oil executive who murmured something in the Santa Barbara oil fiasco should have *run for cover* instead. There are a great many explosive situations, particularly on the public scene in which the press is involved, in which the wise executive will *run for cover* rather than make some of the utterances that he is all too frequently tempted to make to try to defend his position. Remarks intended to be cute or to minimize the seriousness of a situation are frequently a grave tactical error and only serve to infuriate one's adversaries.

This does not mean that the administrator needs to stay under cover, for many times he simply needs to wait until the storm blows over. The tactic is particularly advantageous to use when a highly emotional adversary comes onto the scene who, because of his state of mind, cannot be reasoned with. If the administrator cannot cope with the immediate situation because of such circumstances, then it is wise to *run for cover* until the storm is over. To try to oppose the emotional individual would only be throwing gasoline on the fire.

CLEAR OUT—FOLD THE ENTERPRISE

There comes a time when the only intelligent tactic an administrator can employ in a situation is to clear out—fold the enterprise. He has no hope of victory and to stay and fight will only see him destroyed. It is indeed an intelligent man who knows when to fold his cards in a game. There are several advantages to this tactic. First, it may conserve resources; there's no use wasting ammunition in a lost battle. Second, some unknown observers may be impressed by the wisdom of the administrator who knows when to quit.

Sometimes it means resigning a position. Sometimes it means dropping a product, selling off a division, selling a losing company, selling a bad investment, or cancelling a plan of action. These things can be painful, difficult because of the administrator's ego involvement. We just do not like to fold an enterprise. This tactic is close to the oft given advice, "never send good money after bad," which is one of the basic tenets of any good investor or businessman. Folding is not surrendering; you don't give the adversary that satisfaction. Disguise your action in some manner.

BE THE FALL GUY

Sometimes the wise administrator will deliberately take the blame for something, whether or not he is guilty, in order to ingratiate himself with a superior or to gain the gratitude of a guilty subordinate. It is a big man who admits guilt for something for which he is responsible; he who takes the blame for something for which he is innocent may be even bigger. It can gain allies and buy future favors.

This tactic should be used only in minor matters where, by assuming the guilt, the administrator risks nothing. His action is only a symbol of his "greatness." The opportunity for such symbolic gestures arises many times each day in the many little confusions and misunderstandings that arise during the normal course of the business day.

Your secretary makes a mistake in a letter; "I'm sorry, Jane, I must have given you the wrong spelling of his name." And who knows, perhaps you did.

SUBVERT

While the ethics of this tactic can certainly be questioned, still it is a tactic that some administrators use. Its ethics can only be evaluated within the context of how it is used. There are times when the administrator finds it necessary to destroy his adversary from within. Sometimes he does this by gaining the adversary's confidence and working from within to gain his way, while at other times he has spies or cohorts within the organization. Sometimes the administrator pretends to defend the adversary in order to neutralize him and keep him from being forewarned of an impending plan.

Sometimes this tactic actually involves espionage and the undermining of the adversary's operations in some manner. This tactic is an exceedingly dangerous one to use for if the administrator is discovered, he may be destroyed. There is general contempt in the business world for the employment of subversion. Also, if the administrator has allies in his subversion, he lays himself open for blackmail at a later time. Thereafter, he is vulnerable to the allies' whims. It should take an extreme situation, almost a desperate one, before an administrator should resort to this tactic.

LET THEM SET THEIR OWN SENTENCE

Frequently a subordinate has erred in his ways and, in a manner of speaking, is before you for sentencing. At times it may be wise to allow him to set his own sentence, rather than your doing it, for it may take some of the inevitable bitterness from the discipline if the man has established his own punishment. Sometimes you are placed in the advantageous position of being able to lighten a subordinate's self-imposed punishment, for he has been too severe with himself. This can, of course, transform a somewhat sullen subordinate into a grateful one.

Care should be taken to phrase your request for self-sentencing so that you are not automatically obligated to accept the subordinate's self-sentencing if you strongly disagree with the outcome.

A salesman was caught falsifying his call reports. Company policy was as usual somewhat vague as to what should be done in such matters but it was understood that the manager could fire him if he so desired. But he did not so desire for the man was a good producer. However, some discipline was required for the rest of the men were watching to see what the rules of the game were to be and the manager did want accurate reports from his men. So he called the man into his office and presented him with his dilemma. "Jim. I'll not fire you for I value your services highly, but I must not let this serious infraction of our policies go unnoticed for it may give the rest of the men the wrong idea. Think about it for a few days and then write me a memo on what you think I should do about it. Set your own punishment." In itself this tactic is punishment enough alone for it places a great burden on the man's back.

A few days later the memo came, "Raise my sales quota $20,000 for the year and disqualify me from the present contest we are running." The manager modified the sentence by leaving the man's sales quota alone since it would have cost him a good deal of money.

RIGHTEOUS INDIGNATION

Occasionally there comes a time when the administrator should display righteous indignation over some event. While the normal demeanor of the mature executive is usually that of the cool, calm, and collected mature intellect, sometimes such behavior fails to communicate precisely how one feels about some event to someone who badly needs the message. The tactic can only be used when the administrator is obviously totally in the right and the adversary has committed a wrong that cannot be allowed to go unnoticed.

The president of a small sporting goods manufacturing company had previously warned his personnel manager to stop being so friendly with the various female employees, but the man's indiscretions continued. The president's wrath descended upon the subordinate when precipitated by the complaint of a newly hired young lady of considerable pulchritude, who objected to some of the conditions that were being placed upon her continued employment. The president summoned the errant Don Juan to his office and loudly and emphatically fired him after reading the riot act to him about his misconduct. It was not accidental that the president left the door to his office wide open during the conversation.

Everyone in the office could hear the president's controlled rage, for he wanted to make certain that not only did all other male employees in the company who might be harboring lecherous intentions receive the message loud and clear, but he also wished the girls to be assured of his policy on such matters.

There is very little an adversary can really do in the face of righteous indignation which is based on incontestable facts. However, care must be taken that the adversary is fully deserving of the wrath and that he has no acceptable defense, for if he does, a real shouting match may ensue. Wrongful indignation will beget righteous indignation in return.

The executive should take care that he not use this tactic except very infrequently, lest he garner a reputation for being of unstable temperament.

SILENCE—MAINTAIN YOUR CONFIDENCES

This is a badly under-used tactic, for most men seem to talk too much for their own good and fail to maintain confidences given them. It is a safe assumption that if you say something you do not want somebody else to hear, that information will almost automatically gravitate to that party. Indeed, one of the worst reputations one can develop is that of talking too much. Seldom is one criticized for saying too little.

Let us understand clearly the overpowering force that makes men talk too much in spite of knowing better, for usually they do know better, but for various reasons simply are unable to control their better judgment. First, the bitter truth is that talking is fun. It is social intercourse and man, being a highly social animal, is strongly predisposed toward making noises. The real art lies in being able to make noises without really saying much, yet not having the other party perceive that he is being conversationally shortchanged. Second, people who are insecure about their position frequently feel compelled to impress others of their importance and status by the spoken word. This, of course, is a tragic mistake. Seldom can anyone gain status and prestige through what he says. Status is usually achieved through one's deeds and what others say of you, but the temptation to shorten the road to position is strong and people will continually undertake to impress others through conversation. Third, many men feel a strong compulsion to make others think that they are on the inside, or are in-on-the-know; they talk in order to impress others about how smart they are. It seldom works. Violations of this tactic are so numerous that illustrations are hardly needed.

ACT, DON'T REACT

The president of a leading university developed the unfortunate reputation among his subordinates of being an extremely weak administrator, inasmuch as he constantly reacted to situations rather than acting on them. Eventually he was forced to resign. He habitually waited until he was confronted with a situation caused by others and then he would react to that situation in some manner rather than formulating some plans and programs before such situations developed so that they could be handled within the context of his policies. The problem of always being in a position of reacting is that adversaries, once learning of that propensity of the administrator, will keep creating situations for him to react to. Amid all of these reactions, he finds himself giving way to the pressures of expediency to the long run disadvantage of his policy. A weak administrator tends to try to get out of the immediate situation in the most expedient manner possible, but in doing so he creates situations which he will regret thereafter.

Many university presidents, in dealing with student groups, have shown their weaknesses in just such situations. Instead of having firm, clear cut policies with which to handle incidents as they arise, they have tended to deal with each student group as the situation arises, making policies and rules as the occasion demands.

DON'T ACT FROM EMOTION

An emotional mind is an unthinking one. Seldom does one make sound decisions when emotionally disturbed because emotions block out rational thought. For this reason, the administrator is strongly advised to never act in emotion; instead, he should only act after cold, rational thought. This is closely tied to the tactic of "Act, Don't React".

The president of a manufacturing company learned that one of his directors had taken it upon himself to perform certain operating functions in new product planning. He had contacted some potential competitors to learn something of the business. The president felt this was unethical and reacted somewhat emotionally to it, thereby permanently alienating the director. The director felt the president's behavior was ridiculous.

The president of one closely-held mercantile concern became extremely angry with one of his associates and suddenly severed all relationships by activating a stock repurchase contract they had signed. This proved to be a most serious mistake, for the men were involved in a very complex legal entanglement concerning several of their investments which demanded complete loyalty and unity among them. Once the emotional merchant had kicked his associate out of bed, their interests were in direct opposition. In the end, the emotional outburst cost the merchant about $30,000 that could have been avoided, had he kept his temper with the associate until it was all over and then parted company with him.

TEST THE WATER

Sometimes the administrator is wise if he tests the temperature of the organizational water before he introduces a plan. If the organization reacts adversely to it, he may revise his intentions, but if it is receptive he proceeds to implement the plan.

This is a sound administrative tactic, for little is lost by trying it. The personnel manager of a large manufacturing plant entertained thoughts of staggering the working hours of all workers in order to relieve the traffic congestion in the area during the morning and evening rush hours. Before officially putting forth his idea, he quietly tested it both on the workers and on top management. He quickly encountered vigorous opposition, so he dropped the idea, thereby saving face, for if he had proposed the plan he would have looked rather foolish when it was turned down.

Sometimes the administrator, if he truly wants to disguise the source of an idea while testing the water, may attribute the idea to someone else, an unidentified party, thereby removing his own personal status from the idea, should it be soundly defeated.

LAUGH IT OFF

One rather devastatingly deceptive tactic that an administrator can use to dismiss some criticism or complaint from an adversary is to laugh it off or to treat it as if he were joking; not be serious about his comment. Many times the adversary will quickly fold his tent by pretending that he really was kidding, whereas in fact he was not. This tactic is particularly appropriate when the adversary's criticism is so extreme that one would be justified in assuming that he was kidding. Laughter can be a devastating defensive weapon to be used when one doesn't wish to discuss something seriously. One can laugh off a topic and and then change the subject.

Laughing is a particularly good defense when one really has no answer to give. A bit of laughter combined with silence can leave an adversary completely perplexed and disarm him by your apparent unconcern about the matter. A particularly aggressive door-to-door saleswoman was attempting a last ditch close to sell a set of encyclopedias after an evening of failing to convince a particularly tough prospect. As she was departing, she made her last ditch close by saying, "Well, I'm highly disappointed this evening. I came here expecting to meet a highly intelligent individual, someone interested in the welfare and education of his children. I see I was wrong!"

The worldly-wise prospect just laughed and asked, "How many times does that last ditch effort work for you?"

She chuckled, "Oh, about one time in ten it gets me back in the door."

A holder of a businessman's note had legally exercised its acceleration clause to demand full payment of it when the maker was tardy with a payment. After paying off the note, the businessman was furious at his former creditor and ordered him never to set foot in his place of business again. The ex-creditor left, doubled over with laughter, to the great distress of his adversary who was left standing in the middle of his store shaking his fists in a rage over being laughed at.

A personnel agent was deliberately needling an applicant for an executive job to see how well he took the stress. He needled, "What's the matter? Don't you believe in shining your shoes?", upon noticing that the applicant's shoes were not polished.

The applicant laughed and replied, "I guess I'd better get my wife trained better, hadn't I?"

This neatly parried the personnel manager's thrust and showed that the man had poise. Laughter eases tensions and allows a man time to think of replies. It can sometimes ease the tension in a sticky situation, much to the advantage of all. It is indeed an exceptional administrator who can see the humor of a situation sufficiently that he can laugh at it.

Laughing at the wrong time or in the wrong place can label one either a fool or a buffoon, for there are times and places where laughter is inappropriate and not appreciated by people attempting to solve a serious problem.

IGNORE THE STATIC

In implementing many plans the administrator must learn to ignore outside static being given him by adversaries and push on to a successful culmination of the plan. He should not allow himself to be deterred by minor assaults on his flanks and various noises being made by adversaries. He must figuratively wear ear muffs and blinders so that all he can see are the goals he wishes to achieve and the plan of action by which he hopes to achieve them.

The president of a candy company that traditionally made high quality candies sold through wholesalers to various dealers decided that the future of his company should be to develop a large chain of company-owned retail stores through which it would sell its fine candies directly to the consumer. He was fought on every front by his board of directors, his subordinates, his bankers, and his family. No one agreed with him. But he was extremely strong as a leader so by sheer force of his personality, and the ownership of the majority of the common stock of the company, he executed his plan of action to a phenomenally successful conclusion. He was right and his critics were wrong. Of course, if he had been wrong, he would have looked like a pig-headed fool; it is a risky tactic.

Once an administrator has made up his mind to do something despite what anyone else says or does, then he must develop a mental shield which will help him ignore the static that will be coming his way.

This tactic is particularly advised in handling minor, petty, trivial irritations. It does a great administrator no service to deign to answer petty criticisms. One of the best ways to put down such adversaries is simply to ignore them pointedly as if they were inconsequential.

LET 'EM BITCH

Some administrators deliberately set up sessions at which their subordinates can voice their feelings concerning some plan of action, not with the thought in mind that they are necessarily going to change the plan one iota because of what is said, but just to allow the people to get the frustrations and feelings out of their systems.

The Denver School Board was instituting a plan for busing students to even up racial balance in schools and it finally made up its mind to go ahead with the program. But first it held an open meeting at which it promised everyone would be heard who wanted to speak. The session lasted six hours—into the wee hours of the morning—and more than 150 people spoke for and against the plan. It was quite a spectacle and a good many people probably felt better afterwards for having vented their feelings. In the end, the Board went ahead and voted for the plan that they were going to vote for right along.

An administrator must be certain that he has absolute control over a situation and that such sessions will not get out of control and result in jeopardizing his position.

THE HOT POTATO

Some issues are such potentially explosive situations that the wise administrator avoids being connected with them. He passes the hot potato on to other people. One could question the wisdom of President Nixon in taking on the hot potato of rescinding the route allocation of the Pacific airlines decision made by President Johnson. This was a situation in which somebody was bound to be angry, and they were mad at President Johnson for his initial route allocations. President Nixon, by opening up the decision once again, deliberately took the hot potato in his own hands and reaped the resultant criticism. Evidently he felt that the benefits would exceed the drawbacks.

Administrators in public positions must become quite adept at not allowing hot potatoes to be dumped into their laps for they will inevitably be burned, no matter how well they handle it. Pity the administrator—such as Mayor John Lindsay of New York—who continually has hot potatoes of the greatest magnitude dumped into his lap day after day.

This tactic is closely akin to passing the buck; the difference is that sometimes the administrator does not have to pass a hot potato on, but can merely avoid having it dumped in his lap—now is not the time to become involved with that hot issue.

EYEBALL TO EYEBALL

The late President Kennedy used the eyeball to eyeball tactic in his handling of the Cuban missile crisis in which he met Khrushchev "eyeball to eyeball" and forced him to back down from his aggressive gambit in Cuba.

The business administrator at times will have use for this tactic in displaying firm resolution in standing up for his rights or plans, whether or not he actually has the force to back up his stand or not.

It should be made clear that one does not necessarily have to have the requisite power to exercise the eyeball to eyeball tactic, for it may be a bluff.

This tactic is advised in situations where adversaries are attempting a gambit with the idea in mind that the administrator does not have a firm resolution in the matter. The eyeball to eyeball tactic is aimed to counter this notion among the adversaries.

PUT IT IN WRITING

Suppose an adversary walks into your office with a sudden demand or plan about which you are either uncertain or oppose; one tactic is to ask him to put his request in writing. This gives you time to think about it, makes the adversary think through his position, possibly cools him off or encourages him to modify his demands, and it gets the adversary on paper, which may later prove to be highly advantageous for the document may prove to be his undoing.

As a general rule, having one's adversaries put plans or criticisms in writing is a very sound one. Sometimes merely requesting that a subordinate put something in writing thwarts his entire gambit. This can be either good or bad. It is bad if it stifles initiative or otherwise blocks off sound ideas.

LET'S DO RESEARCH

One stalling tactic, which at times is unassailable, is to suggest that additional research needs to be done on a proposal. This always sounds so reasonable that many times it is difficult for the adversary to overcome it and get immediate action. Naturally many proposals die in the research stage where an adroit administrator can manage to have them buried by the selection of who is to do the research and how much is to be spent on it.

This tactic is kissing cousin to *The Stall* but with a difference—there is a seemingly sound reason for this delay. It is surprising how many ideas are dampened by this maneuver for the adversary is quite apt to write off further pursuit of his plan as being a waste of time. And he is probably correct for the administrator will most likely locate another tactic to forestall an unwanted plan.

The research ploy can also be used to pass the buck onto other shoulders. Ford was wont to blame its Edsel fiasco on faulty research, research that was largely ignored by management. A particularly costly, and most enterprising, program for marketing wood products by a large lumber company was in difficulty. Its project manager called for a research study to determine the difficulty. He had not the slightest intention of really listening to the study's findings and recommendations but rather was playing the standard game played by all executives in this company to cover themselves when called upon by the board of directors to explain their mismanagement of their program. Woe to the program manager who had not asked for research to assist him. But the manager who could show that he had done his homework, had the research performed, had no fear for he would be let off the hook as having done everything that could be expected of him. After all if research can't save the day, how can mere mortals be expected to do better?

REFER TO A COMMITTEE

One of the classic stalling tactics of an administrator is to refer a proposal or plan submitted by an adversary with which he is not in accord to a committee for further study. This can be an effective tactic to use, particularly when organizational policy clearly calls for it to be given to some committee. Committees can be an asset in helping the administrator control the dimensions and characteristics of plans if he has control over the membership of the committees.

If he does not have control over a committee, the use of this tactic can be risky, for he may not like the committee's recommendations. Also, this tactic can infuriate adversaries who are fully aware of what is going on. If their permanent alienation is not desirable, the use of this tactic may work to the long run detriment of the administrator. He can become known as a man who cannot make a decision for himself.

HAVE A FALL GUY!

It is usually best for one's career not to have the blood stains of a disaster fall directly on one's shoulders. Most plans of action entail some risk of disaster; in such cases, particularly where the risks are high, the wise administrator may arrange to have a scapegoat handy. An executive vice president of a manufacturing company was most interested in developing a certain new product which entailed considerable market risk. He spotted a bright young junior executive who was also highly interested in the product and let the young man believe that the product's idea was his own and that it would provide the young man with a tremendous opportunity for advancement in the organization, should he be able to pull off the new product introduction successfully. When the product failed, no criticism was aimed at the executive vice president, for he was apparently free from direct responsibility. He had seen to it that the entire responsibility for the new product rested on the shoulders of the product manager who, for some odd reason, found himself seeking new employment.

This tactic has little risk if it is done with sufficient subtlety. Success in most large corporations depends on the adept execution of this tactic for the key to advancement is to never be left holding the bag or be fully responsible for some corporate disaster. If one can but keep his nose clean for the requisite number of years, his advancement is assured.

EXILE TO SIBERIA

Sometimes an administrator is in a position to physically move an adversary; exile him, so that he is rendered relatively impotent. At times this can be done disguised as a promotion; the adversary is offered a promotion to some remote spot in the organization where he will cause the administrator little future trouble.

The dean of one School of Business was bothered by one troublesome professor who was continually creating one problem or another. Inasmuch as the university had several campuses, and it was completely within the dean's discretion to determine the man's teaching assignment, he simply assigned the man to a remote small campus, thereby isolating him geographically.

Sometimes being exiled does not require a geographical move, but merely an organizational one. The top management of a large corporation had a particularly troublesome middle management man who was too aggressive for their conservative tastes. Since the man had an outstanding record of productivity, they could not fire him without many questions being asked. However, his immediate superior conned him into accepting a promotion to head up a troublesome division within the company, but it was a quagmire—a quagmire that contained the remains of a great many promising managerial careers. After doing an admirable job with the division, the young executive finally became fed up with its unsolvable problems and resigned, to the silent relief of the conservative higher management.

ON PERSONAL RELATIONSHIPS

Many of the daily tactics the administrator uses concern his relationships with his subordinates, peers, and superiors. Indeed, his success in the organization is largely determined by how adroitly he handles these relationships for if he fails to develop them properly he is lost.

Usually the administrator is friendly with his peers for they are really the only people in the organization with whom he can socialize comfortably. But one can encounter problems with peer relationships. There are always competitive jealousies lurking on the horizon that one must guard against. And then there is the administrator who is on the way up and knows it. He had best not form too close of a relationship with his peers who one day will be his subordinates. Ever fire a friend, discipline a buddy? Personal involvement with one's subordinates inserts an element into the decision process that warps the results. The able administrator must select his peer-group friends carefully. Pick the winners, avoid the losers: You are judged by the company you keep. Associate with the people who are going places, doing things.

People are frequently unhappy that they are unable to develop the close personal relationships with others that they had during their school years. But that is not to be in most circumstances for the gloried innocent days of childhood are largely a product of a wistful memory.

Although many superiors encourage close relationships with their subordinates, from the subordinate's viewpoint the relationship is difficult and dangerous for he is on the spot constantly and must be careful of everything he says and does. Moreover, should the subordinate try to make too much of the personal relationship, capitalize upon it, he may discover the boss's goodwill not to be what he had been lead to believe.

Friendliness on the part of the boss is often misconstrued. It may be his natural personality or an effort on his part to get to know his people better, to be human. He may not intend that it go any further.

The man who develops a close relationship with his boss will be subject to a certain amount of resentment, and various tactics, by others in the organization who are either jealous or who want to destroy the relationship.

Admittedly, there are superiors who are lonely. They

crave a close relationship with somebody, somebody in whom they can place trust, somebody who can act as a sounding board, somebody who can be a playmate. But it is dangerous for a subordinate to try to play this role. Only in rare instances will it work out successfully.

And then there are the bosses who demand that subordinates keep their distance, call them "Mister," treat them with exaggerated respect. If one of these belongs to you, then you had best be most circumspect in your contacts with him. And there are far more of these men around than is obvious on the surface for modern social pressures have forced such traditionalists to apparently change their attitudes. Do not be deceived by their apparent behavior for at heart they still want the symbols of respect they think are due their position. Give it to them!

And now what about your subordinates? There are advantages to being close to your men. You have better communications with them. You can evaluate them more accurately. They should respond to your leadership more readily. But what is "close"? Where does "close" stop and "intimate" begin? It is a most difficult line to draw but it must be drawn for there are grave dangers awaiting the boss who becomes an intimate friend with a subordinate. One of the problems is that one can not be equally close to all of his men so inevitably some of them feel discriminated against. The answers to these questions depend upon a good many factors such as the personalities of the boss and the men, their relative social backgrounds, the size of the organization, and the caliber of the men.

As you can now see I have no answers to these questions of your personal relationships in business, only warnings and a few observations.

2

TIMING TACTICS

Timing is of the essence in the maneuvers of most administrators. Deciding when to take action can be just as critical in the final outcome of a plan as the substance of the plan itself. And so consideration must be given to timing tactics.

Underlying most timing tactics is the matter of the mental attitude of one's adversaries at the time. A person's reaction to any action is heavily conditioned by all the things that have happened to him previously, particularly in the immediate past. If the boss's wife has just filed suit for divorce, it is not the time to ask him for a raise, or much of anything else.

LEAVE WELL ENOUGH ALONE

It takes an administrator of great wisdom and patience to be able to keep his hands off a situation that is bothering him, but sometimes that is precisely what he must do—nothing. Sometimes this is the proper tactic to use because nothing can be done about a situation; the administrator is helpless to correct it and his meddling will do nothing but either worsen the situation or jeopardize his position. In other cases the matter is none of his affair; it is the responsibility of some other administrator and he had better not interfere.

Sometimes a situation is such that it is simply not serious enough to warrant the administrator's spending his time with it; for the sake of efficiency, he should leave it alone. This is particularly true in some situations in which the amount of time required would be relatively large in comparison with the profits achievable. One top executive once said, "If ten troubles come down the road at you and you just stand still, nine of them will fall by the wayside and you'll only have to deal with the one that reaches you." Some problems take care of themselves. A troublesome employee may resign, retire, or request a transfer.

Sometimes the administrator may not be happy about some action or program developed by a subordinate, but he should refrain from interfering with it for three reasons: (1) allowing subordinates freedom without interference can facilitate their development and growth; (2) there is no assurance that the administrator's thoughts would be superior to those of the subordinate; and, (3) the program is apt to be more successful if the people responsible for implementing it have developed it.

A leading salesman for a large furniture manufacturer had been promoted to sales manager. He had been aware of several problems in the alignment of sales territories. While he wanted to straighten out the sales territories, he wisely deferred this action for it was not really hurting sales volume and to juggle the territorial boundaries upon assumption of his managership might have caused some morale problems and jeopardized some other programs he wished to institute.

The administrator must take care that the problems he leaves alone will not later become uncontrollable or unmanageable. The president of a large university had a problem with an editor of the student newspaper who insisted on printing articles libeling various important people. In the name of academic freedom, the president refrained from acting until he was forced to do so. He eventually fired the editor, but it was too late to save his own job for he was also fired shortly thereafter.

An administrator may have to act in spite of his believing that he should leave well enough alone. If his organization feels that something definitely must be done about a situation, he may have to make some moves for reasons of morale.

CHOOSE YOUR TIME

Timing is critical in the execution of most plans. In fact, a case can be made that the success or failure in any gambit may depend more upon its timing than upon any other single factor. An executive wishes to hire a highly capable man away from a competitor. Whether or not he gets that man may depend upon the timing of his proposition. Almost inevitably there are times in the life of anyone in which he is receptive to job offers.

Obviously, the administrator attempts to choose a time in which the adversary is either most susceptible to suggestion or a time at which he is unable to defend himself most ably.

A businessman may be unwilling to negotiate some financial matter in realistic terms at a time when he feels prosperous, but should his fortunes turn for the worse he may be far more reasonable in his demands. The converse may also be true, depending on his personality. One white collar worker learned that a bank had just given a local car dealer an ultimatum to clear out some car inventory that had been in stock far too long; he was able to approach the dealer immediately and buy a new car on quite advantageous terms, whereas three months previously the dealer had been unreasonable in his price demands. Timing is frequently everything in price negotiations.

Sometimes the timing tactic is closely akin to the stall. In stalling, the administrator does everything in his power to prolong an affair because the situation is such that with the passing of time he gains bargaining power; either his strength is increasing or the adversary's is decreasing. One large automobile dealer, in advising a fellow dealer about a dispute with a bank over some installment paper that went bad, advised, "Everytime I have a hassle with my banker, I just make a mental note that we'll settle it in about three years. There is no hurry about it. Just don't take any action at all. Let the bank initiate all the action and do all the moving. You remain passive. They'll keep kicking it around between junior executives, with each one taking about six months before he does anything and before you know it, three years have passed and somebody down there will make up their mind that they had better settle it. So they'll come to you and will be quite reasonable. But if you rush in trying to get this thing settled, you'll lose all your advantage."

BE PATIENT—BIDE YOUR TIME

Recently an outstanding lawyer voiced this opinion in a casual conversation: "I believe that in all my legal experience with business that probably the single most important virtue a good businessman can have is patience. Many things simply take time and the man who is impatient inevitably commits mistakes to his disadvantage. It takes time to build empires and get things done and the impatient man is at a distinct disadvantage." Good advice! This tends to be particularly applicable to young businessmen who are impatient to get ahead with things, figuring a way to accomplish things in a short while and becoming impatient with those who seem to slow them down. It takes time to get situations straightened around and clarified. Many times the winner in a contest is the one who outlives the other, or out-stays him. Many older executives simply bury their adversaries. A dean of a School of Business took over a situation in which several older professors were thorns in his side, delaying several progressive programs he would have liked to begin. However, he decided that since the men were near retirement age that most of his problems would be solved within five years. Rather than risking a frontal attack on the situation, he simply bided his time until they retired and then went ahead with his programs.

Unfortunately, time is of the essence and in biding one's time, opportunities are lost forever and one adversary can be substituted for another. Patience may be the mask of a timid man.

LET THE SITUATION WORSEN

Occasionally the best one can do is to let a bad situation get worse, for if he acts too soon he will be criticized as taking unwarranted action. President Roosevelt had to use this tactic in instituting rationing during World War II. He had to let a situation get sufficiently difficult before the public would accept rationing; if he had acted any earlier, he would have encountered considerable resistance from the public.

There are some dangers in using this tactic, for some situations may worsen to the point where an administrator cannot straighten out the mess, thereby causing losses. It takes great forbearance to let a situation worsen to a point where action can be taken. A sales manager had a salesman in a particularly critical territory who at one time was one of the company's leading performers, but who had been slipping steadily in recent years. This salesman had many friends throughout the company and was well liked. While the sales manager, from a strictly managerial standpoint, had ample reason to discharge the man for his failing performance, to do so would have created a serious morale problem in the organization. He was forced to sit by for two years until the man's performance became so shoddy that everyone in the organization was aware of it. When the sales manager finally discharged the man, the organization's general consensus was, "Why wasn't it done earlier?"

STRIKE WHILE THE IRON IS HOT

The age-old tactic almost speaks for itself. The aggressive, alert administrator must strike when it is highly advantageous for him to do so, regardless of all other factors, because the success of his plan may depend more upon the existence of fortunate timing than any other factor in the situation.

Naturally, the administrator must make certain that the time is hot and that when he strikes he has sufficient resources with which to do the job. A fifty-five year old treasurer of a medium sized corporation was offered the controllership of a large prestigious organization. He hesitated and then turned it down. Within a few months the situation in his company was completely altered by a merger. He contacted the larger firm again, only to find that they were no longer interested in him. Apparently neither was anyone else, so he had to stay in an unhappy position.

STRIKE WHEN YOU'RE STRONG

At times the administrator is wise if he postpones making his move until he is sufficiently strong or ready to execute it successfully. The president of a small university was particularly desirous of building up a doctoral program in one of the sciences, but he had to delay introduction of his program for three years while he was garnering manpower and resources to make the program successful when introduced. To have announced the program earlier and to have accepted students into it would have jeopardized its long run success.

However, some of the famous military disasters in history were caused by leeaders who waited and waited until they felt they were sufficiently strong for the plan at hand; they were undone by the delay. Timid leaders frequently like to use this tactic as a cover up for their timidity in instances where such strength is really not necessary for the plan. One seldom has the resources he thinks he should have to execute a plan successfully.

STRIKE WHEN IT HURTS THE ADVERSARIES

Adversaries can be hurt worse at some times more than at others. If plans call for inflicting maximum damage on the foe, the timing of the plan should be such that it hurts them most. While this tactic has far more application to the military than to business, still it does have some industrial applications. One appliance manufacturer chose a time when a significant competitor's plant was on strike to launch a sales program designed to increase his number of distributors and dealers in the hope that it could take away some of the competitor's dealers who were unhappy at being unable to obtain supplies from the strike-bound plant.

DON'T LET THEM DIG IN

Speed is frequently essential in actions, lest the adversary gain a toehold or be able to solidify its position, thereby presenting a stronger counterforce at a later date. When the Wilkinson Sword Company introduced its stainless steel double-edged shaving blade into the U.S. market a few years ago, the management of Gilette correctly saw that it would have to counter this move quickly to prevent Wilkinson's gaining a permanently large share of the market. Bon Ami, on the other hand, allowed Ajax and Glasswax to take away its markets with new products and aggressive advertising; it was three or four years in counterattacking which failed miserably, thereby leading to the ultimate downfall of the company.

The major problem, which must be guarded against in exercising this tactic, is that in one's haste to strike he may devise a faulty plan. It is all too easy to rush off half cocked to strike either at some undeserving problem or to strike improperly at the real problem.

3

NEGOTIATING AND PERSUASIVE TACTICS

One of the least discussed functions of the administrator is that of negotiation. One of the surprises in store for the would-be top executive is the amount of time he will spend in negotiation; he will be constantly negotiating with somebody for something or other. He negotiates with bankers and investment brokers for money. He negotiates with labor unions over wage rates. He negotiates with the market over the price of his product. He negotiates with his subordinates over wages and other demands. He negotiates with suppliers for lower prices and landlords for lower rents. He negotiates with property owners for the sale of property; he negotiates with the government over taxes and other legal matters. Since the administrator constantly negotiates, his ultimate success almost completely depends upon his negotiating skills. The inept negotiator will always pay too much and get too little, thus being rendered competitively weak.

An administrator is also continually trying to persuade someone to do something; this is the essence of implementing a plan. Once a plan has been formulated, the administrator must persuade, by one means or another, all parties necessary to the plan to carry out their parts of it. Persuasion can be a difficult task, for the parties may not always wish to cooperate.

Actually, you should realize that persuasion and nego tiation are closely related tactical categories, for the essence of negotiation is to persuade the adversary to accept your terms.

NARROWING THE FIELD

Early in negotiations one should endeavor to narrow the areas of disagreement between himself and the adversary so that there are disagreements on as few points as possible. In these early stages the parties should determine the areas in which they are in complete agreement and sign off those areas as agreed upon, leaving them closed thereafter. This is known as erecting roadblocks or barriers, so that in later stages the adversary cannot come back and reopen these decided matters when he feels he is not getting his way in the areas of dispute. The field has been narrowed to as few points of dispute as possible; then negotiations can get underway on each point. It is advisable to focus negotiations on one point at a time, rather than wandering from point to point in confusion.

THE BLANK CHECK

The faculty of one business school felt a strong desire to change its curriculum rather radically. Perhaps it felt that any change had to be for the better, but no matter, the desire was so overwhelming that they decided to do something about it. Long experience had painfully proved the impossibility of getting two professors to agree on anything so complex as an entire curriculum, let alone a whole faculty. Any committee recommendations that would be brought before the faculty would be so chopped up before passed that the end result would be pitiful. So the faculty granted the curriculum committee a blank check beforehand. They passed a motion that the committee had the power to institute a new curriculum without coming to the faculty for approval. Most unusual. A most interesting tactic.

If you are assigned some delicate or controversial task and do not wish to waste your time doing something that will come to naught when brought before a higher authority, then try to get a *blank check* to execute your plan without further authority. If your power is sufficient, your stand should be: no blank check, no work. One can not easily do this in most work situations, but the tactic is quite applicable in other affairs. A Little League board asks you to head up the umpires; get a blank check to run the operation as you see fit with no second guessing from the board. The time to get the blank check is before you undertake the task or the job. Get the authority you need and want before accepting the job.

BAIT YOUR HOOK

You can't catch fish with a bare hook; if you want to reel in a prize fish you must bait your hook with the proper enticement. The easiest way to get somebody to do something you want them to do is to make it worth their while. It is amazing the number of administrators that do not seem to understand this basic principle of motivation. They frequently expect the other person to do something out of the kindness of his heart or just because he is ordered to do it. If you really want somebody to do something, make sure you give him a good reason for doing it. Such things as bonuses, pay raises, vacations, or something else the adversary wants (possibly continued employment) can all be used as effective bait.

A large building contractor was having a difficult time persuading the authorities to grant him some much needed zoning variances. He gained his way by baiting the hook with a small land grant to the city for a long desired park in the area.

There are really no adverse aspects to the use of this tactic, except that at times one my put too much bait on the hook, thereby increasing the cost of the plan beyond acceptability.

DISGUISE TRUE DESIRES

An age-old horsetrading tactic is to never let the seller know which horse it is that the buyer is interested in, for the price on it will immediately go up if the seller is aware. The adept buyer goes to great lengths to disguise his true interests. This means that the truly important negotiating factors may not come up first but sometimes are brought in later as seemingly minor side issues, yet these may be the truly important ones that the other party is most concerned about.

One young man who was negotiating with a potential employer for a job focused most of the negotiations on money to disguise the fact that he had already made up his mind to accept the job because he wanted to live in that particular community. Had his strong desire to live in that area been disclosed to the employer, the man's bargaining position for money would have been completely destroyed and he would have had to accept a much lower salary.

BE YOUR OWN CASTING DIRECTOR

Sometimes men will play the role into which they are cast If you wish them to play a particular role for you, you must be the casting director.

A salesman had been having a most difficult time cracking a particularly large industrial account, largely because of the obstinate behavior of a purchasing agent who strongly favored a competitor. The salesman approached the purchasing agent with the statement, "Sir, from what I have heard about you, you are a most impartial purchasing agent who firmly adheres to the proven policy of maintaining multiple sources of supply on critical items." He tried to cast the purchasing agent into the role he wished him to play.

This tactic is based largely on two psychological forces. First, the laws of suggestion come into play here, as many people will instinctively play the role which has been suggested for them. Second, many people are highly accommodating; they want the other person to like them and are constantly trying to perceive and play the role that is expected of them by the other party. One should never be afraid of playing the role of a casting director for really there is little that can go wrong in applying this tactic if it is done with some finesse and does not run counter to the man's self concepts.

CARRY A BIG STICK

Many staff administrators and assistants to some chief executive accomplish their persuasive ends in the name of their bosses—they carry a big stick; that is, they constantly are carrying with them the authority of their superiors for the subordinates or other executives whom they are attempting to persuade are tacitly threatened with having the assistant report back to his superior that the other party was uncooperative. Many times the staff man opens a conversation with such words as, "the boss would like me to . . ."

A man who continually goes around overtly using the authority of his superior develops feelings of antagonism against himself from his subordinates, for this type of individual is easily disliked with ultimate disaster to himself. If one has enough enemies in the organization, sooner or later they will get him. No one likes to have rank pulled on him, so while this tactic will work a few times, its use should be highly selective.

BRING YOUR OWN EXPERT

Many times the administrator lacks the expertise with which to establish himself as an authority on some matter at issue with an adversary, thereby placing him at a distinct disadvantage in their persuasive maneuverings. In such cases, it is a sound tactic for one to bring his own expert with him to the confrontation, one who's credentials are distinctly superior to those of the adversary.

A newly hired sales manager of a large metals company was having a difficult time persuading the company's controller to change the firm's traditional method for paying the expenses of its salesmen. Previously the company had been paying the men one lump sum for both salary and expenses, thereby forcing the salesmen to differentiate between the two to the satisfaction of the Internal Revenue Service. The sales manager wished to pay them their expenses separately, thereby relieving them of a great deal of book work and difficulties with the income tax men. This was part of the plan he wished to institute for making the sales job easier for the men so that they could devote more time to actually selling the company's products. The controller's reluctance to accommodate the sales manager was largely based on the inconvenience it was going to cause him in changing the company's system, although he did put forth some fallacious legal arguments in hope of quickly bluffing the sales manager out of his plan. The sales manager retained the services of a recognized expert in the field of salesmen's compensation and expenses. The sales manager introduced the controller to his expert, citing all of his credentials and writings which clearly established him as an authority in the field. The meeting progressed into the matter of paying salesmen's expenses. For some strange reason, all of the arguments the controller had previously been putting forth seemed to evaporate in a short ten minute session during which the sales manager was able to have his complete way on the matter. The controller put forth some legal defenses, only to be refuted by the expert who cited the Revenue Code with a great deal of authority.

Many times an adversary will try to bluff you if he knows that you are uninformed in an area, but his bluff is called if you have your own expert to examine his cards carefully.

SET UP STRAW MEN

An age-old negotiating tactic is to set up straw men for the adversary to knock down, thereby leading him to believe that he won a victory. A straw man is some demand or condition that the administrator puts forth solely for the opposition to knock down; he is not at all serious about the straw man and fully expects it to be annihilated, but he fully intends to extract his price for allowing the straw man's annihilation. The adept administrator will frequently establish several straw men and, not too surprisingly, if he faces inept adversaries, he may receive some of the requests he did not anticipate.

Typically, clever negotiators slowly probe and test every claim and demand made by their adversaries to see which are straw men and which are hard core demands. Hence, the tough negotiator does not want to give all his straw men away too quickly lest he be discovered and disarmed in the mental battle fought between negotiators.

Naturally, straw men must be logical and have some support lest they be brushed aside lightly by the adversaries with no gain to the administrator.

NOSE IN THE TENT, OR FOOT IN THE DOOR

Another age-old tactic is to settle for small, immediate gains in certain areas heretofore unpenetrable, in the hope that once the administrator has his nose in the tent he will be able to move in slowly and take over more of the tent. The tactic works surprisingly well. Once a precedent is broken, it is much easier at a later date to negotiate even larger concessions; small concessions lead to larger ones.

Sometimes a consultant will undertake work for a promising client at a relatively attractive price and perform superbly in the hope that he can get his foot in the door, or nose in the tent. Sometimes a company will shave its price or offer special services in order to get a foot in the door of some large potential account.

The basis of success for this tactic is that the first demand must seem so utterly reasonable. Because the administrator seems to want only a very small concession, the adversary is highly tempted to give it to him in the hope that he will be buying permanent peace by doing so. People tend to discount potential future trouble in preference to peace in the present.

LEAVE THE LID ON PANDORA'S BOX or DON'T OPEN UP OLD WOUNDS

There are many occasions in the negotiations between men in which one is tempted to introduce a new subject or reopen one that has been closed. This is an exceedingly dangerous undertaking and should only be done after some thought has been given to it.

If you decide to open up a new area—"take the lid off Pandora's box"—you can never be quite certain what will come out, as your adversary may take the opportunity to enlarge upon his demands or use the new topic as a springboard into some other area. The more factors that you bring into a negotiation, the more difficult you make it. One of the basic tactics in bargaining is to narrow the scope or number of issues involved in the bargaining, and opening up a "Pandora's Box" counters that sound tactic.

SHOOT FOR THE MOON

A standard negotiating tactic is to ask for the moon and settle for less, so that the other party feels he won some sort of victory. Long a favorite tactic of labor union leaders in their negotiating sessions with management, they correctly surmise that they have nothing to lose by using the tactic.

However, in more realistic administrative situations there are some dangers in employing this tactic, for the administrator who is overly dependent upon it will have his demands completely discounted as he becomes known as a moon shooter.

A young administrator who had been offered a particularly challenging job which had many problems made many demands upon management as a condition for his accepting the responsibility. He included in his demands just about everything imaginable that he could possibly need to deal with the problems. While he knew perfectly well that he would not be granted all of his demands, he still made them in the hope of getting as many of them granted as possible. Moreover, he wanted to be on record before accepting the job as to what, in his opinion, it would take to remedy the situation. If he failed in the task, he had created a possible scapegoat—his boss would not give him what he needed to be successful.

RAISE THE STAKES—BUY THE POT

A well recognized principle of poker is to never put your feet under the table with a man richer than yourself for he will then be able to seize pots that are legitimately yours by betting so heavily that your good sense forces you to fold, for you simply can not afford to stay with him—he has bought the pot.

Large organizations lock smaller ones out of certain markets by making the stakes too high for them to afford to even look as some cards in the game. A certain political organization was able to restrict the bidding for large paving contracts to a selected few contractors by making the bonding requirements so high that the smaller contractors could not play the game.

A large electronics manufacturing concern bidding for a sizable defense contract removed one troublesome smaller firm from the picture by an interesting combination of tactics the essence of which was that the price of game became too expensive for the smaller firm. Mr. Big approached Mr. Small with the proposition that if Mr. Small would not bid on the contract, and Mr. Big got it, Mr. Small would be given a subcontract for a sizable section of the work. Moreover, no matter what might happen on the bid, Mr. Small would be given some subcontracting work about which the two concerns had been negotiating for sometime. However, should Mr. Small decline this invitation to collude, Mr. Big would cut off all present subcontracts and investigate the possibility of a patent infringement suit on a matter at dispute between them in another affair. Whee! The price of poker just went up. Mr. Small could not afford to call Mr. Big's hand. Lest the antitrust implications bother you, forget it—it was an international incident.

On the other hand, an administrator must be careful not to raise the stakes of a game so high that his friends and allies can not play with him. One young avid golfing executive had enjoyed excellent relations with several of his peers with whom he played golf weekly at a local municipal course. His fortunes were blessed so he joined a rather expensive country club only to be dismayed that his former friends could no longer stay with him. He was too expensive a playmate for them. Relations between the men were not quite the same thereafter.

LEARN THE ADVERSARY'S LIMITS

The key to successful negotiating is to learn the limits of the other party; i.e., the extent beyond which he will not go. Once the adversary's limits are learned, negotiations become relatively easy for one knows just how far the adversary can be pushed before negotiations will be severed. Once a purchasing agent learns that a salesman will lower his price to a given level, then that is exactly where the bargaining will end up. Conversely, once a salesman learns that a purchasing agent will pay so much, that is where the price will be.

It is most important for the negotiator not only to conceal his own limits, but also to disguise or even mislead the adversary as to exactly what those limits are. Used car salesmen frequently ask the potential buyer what he wants for his old car. It is a mistake to disclose one's price first. Obviously the seller, in most situations, is at a distinct disadvantage because he is required by tradition to quote a price first, which forms the upper limit from which bargaining takes place. Astute horsetraders try to get would-be purchasers to bid before quoting a price, in the hope that the bid will be higher than the intended asking price.

A good deal of the time the seller's lower limits are set by what he can get for his goods elsewhere. If he can make the buyer believe that he has a bona fide offer in his pocket for a certain desired amount, it will force the buyer to either forget about the deal or better the offer. A home owner trying to sell his own home was in an extremely weak bargaining position due to his particular circumstances but he had to have at least $45,000 for his house. So he kept a most official-looking offer from a fictitious buyer handy so that prospective buyers could "accidently" see it on his desk as they wondered through the house. As the house was well worth the money, he was able to set his lower limits rather effectively—he sold for $45,500.

Really, this matter of bargaining rests on the managing of limits—making the other party believe your stated limits and discovering his actual ones.

RUN A BLUFF

The art of bluffing is the essence of negotiation and bargaining. Bluffing is defined as the art of trying to make the adversary believe one holds cards higher than he actually does. The bluff may entail making the adversary think that one has other buyers willing to pay more for something, or it may entail leading one's superior to think that other companies are trying to lure him away.

The art of running a bluff is something unto itself. It requires several of the tactics discussed here, plus an ability to act convincingly and behave persuasively.

There are situations in which it is unwise to run a bluff, for it may be called. One successful football coach made demands for more money after each successful season to the Board of Trustees, using as a lever the bluff that he was going to leave the university for a pro coaching job. Actually, the man had little desire to go into pro ranks. He was well situated in his position and his family was quite happy there. After pulling this holdup game three years in a row, the Board of Trustees finally handed him his hat and said, "It's been nice knowing you!" They called his bluff. The man had no alternative but to accept the pro job, one that he was not particularly happy with. From that point on the story is not very pretty.

Suffice it to say that there are times when the administrator is ill-advised to bluff unless he is prepared to accept the consequences of having his bluff called, for that will happen in most instances. So don't bluff in situations where you can't afford to have the bluff called.

Bluffs are most effective when supported by some visual evidence. In a five card stud game, four spades showing certainly makes for good bluffing material. The same type of evidence is needed to support other bluffs. A young junior executive, whatever that is, wanted more money, more responsibility. But he was hampered in his search for success by the fact that he liked his job, his boss, and did not really want to leave. Moreover, he had good reason to believe that his boss liked him and wanted to keep him. But something had to be done to precipitate some action on his advancement. After reading *The Organization Man,* in which Whyte put forth the correct philosophy that the only way one can really get a raise is through his tacit threat to go elsewhere for employment, he developed a bluff around that bit of information. At an opportune time he asked his boss for advice on a business proposition that had allegedly been made to him which would have resulted in his having to change employers. Thus indirectly he placed the superior on notice that unless some benefits were forthcoming shortly he might go elsewhere for them.

KEEP A TRUMP CARD

In serious negotiations it is highly advantageous to have a trump card to play if needed. One might prefer not to play it unless forced to do so, but at least he should have it to win the game if he feels it is important to do so. A minority stockholder of a small corporation was attempting to get a fair price for his stock in a squeeze-out maneuver being put on him by the majority stockholders. The majority stockholders were trying to cheat him in the deal.

The minority stockholder's trump card was that the majority stockholders had been guilty of many illegal practices, including cheating on their income taxes, and the minority stockholder knew where all the bodies were buried. This was his trump card which he hoped that he would not have to play, but if they did not negotiate a fair settlement he was fully prepared to file suit against them for misuse of corporate assets. However, he had to be very careful not to overtly threaten them with such suits because there are laws dealing with such threats.

Trump cards can be held secretly to be brought out into the open only when needed in the last moments of battle.

There are really no drawbacks to the holding of trump cards. It is just a matter of knowing when and if they should be played. Of course the administrator is never quite certain of what trumps the adversaries hold and whether or not they are higher than his trumps.

THE DOCUMENTED LIE

A most basic tactic in negotiating is the documented lie. Purchasing agents have been known to falsify documents to prove low prices of competitors for the purpose of getting a supplier to meet them—to lower his price, too. The negotiator can prepare all sorts of cost figures and work up substantial documentation to prove that he must get a certain price for his product. Real estate agents have been known to put a larger amount of federal transfer stamps on deeds in order to make future buyers believe that a property sold for a higher price than was actually negotiated.

The purpose of this tactic is to mislead the adversary about your limits. People tend to accept the other fellow's costs as a lower limit since it is fairly well accepted that few people are willing to sell things below cost. So an art of documenting costs has come to the fore in bargaining situations.

As a general rule, people have been trained to believe things that are in writing without questioning their authenticity. Some negotiators, therefore, arrange to have proper documentation for their statements deliberately shown to the adversary, or he is allowed to sneak a look at them at an opportune time. Purchasing agents have been known to leave their offices deliberately to allow a salesman to sneak a look at competitive bids on a desk.

Care should be taken not to be caught in such false documentation in dealing with people with whom you must have future dealings, for this will destroy your effectiveness with them.

THE RED HERRING

In both negotiating and persuading, sometimes the adroit administrator must drag a red herring across the path of the adversary in order to confuse him or divert his attention.

The red herring has defensive overtones, for it is most frequently used in giving false justifications for certain actions when the administrator does not care to reveal the true ones. In many instances it is not wise to reveal the real reasons for undertaking an action; one is frequently best advised to draw a red herring across the path by giving false—but socially acceptable and rational—reasons for the action.

The sales manager ordered a salesman to move from his territory in eastern Pennsylvania to one in Nebraska "in order to bolster up the weak Nebraska territory." The salesman resigned as the manager fully expected him to do, for he knew the man had deep roots in Pennsylvania. the real reason underlying the sales manager's actions was that the man had been a troublemaker and the sales manager wished to get rid of him. It would not do for the real reason to be exposed; a red herring was called for.

Properly executed, the red herring is a fairly safe tactic. Even if the adversaries suspect its existence, there is little they can do except have their suspicions.

BE UNREASONABLE

One expert wrote an article in *Harvard Business Review* on the thesis that the art of being a good negotiator rested on the art of being completely unreasonable; that good negotiators are unreasonable and are able to force unreasonable demands on people who are intimidated by their unreasonableness. Weaker negotiators fail and fall by the wayside. Many labor union leaders use this tactic and sometimes bulldoze their way to better settlements for the membership than would have been possible had they taken a "fair and reasonable" approach.

The use of this tactic can be easily observed in world politics as certain foreign nations take a completely intractable and unreasonable stand for a long period of time until the adversaries are thoroughly convinced nothing can be done with them. Then, and only then do they back down sufficiently that an agreement can be reached. The adversaries in these cases are frequently so happy to get any concessions at all from a situation that was considered completely hopeless that they frequently will grab at a deal that they would have dismissed previously.

This tactic cannot be used to negotiate with people with whom the administrator must continue on a friendly social basis. It is not recommended as a way of making friends. It is strictly a hard-headed negotiating tactic to be used in a few circumstances.

KEEP TALKING

One of the fundamental tactics in all negotiations is to keep talking, no matter how far apart you might be from the adversary. One can see the application of this in the peace councils of the world, in which the adversaries—no matter how antagonistic and far apart their stands may be—still force themselves to come back to the bargaining table week after week to keep talking. As long as people are talking, there is little likelihood of fighting. It seldom pays to sever communications with your adversary if you are trying to bargain with him. This is akin to keeping the door open. Frequently, if one keeps talking with an adversary some basis of a compromise can be worked out or some accommodation can be developed.

There are a few instances in which continued talking may be a disservice to the negotiator. The personalities of some adversaries are such that they disdain talking and view with contempt people who do so; hence, the less said the better in such situations. If the negotiator is taking a firm and reasonable stand on something, continued talks may indicate a willingness to compromise, which he wishes to avoid giving.

One danger in talking so much during a negotiation is that one may disclose things during the discourse that would have preferably remained secret. One big advantage to a negotiator in encouraging the adversary to talk is that he may learn some valuable information that will give him the upper hand.

STALL

Time is frequently an important factor in the final outcome of a negotiation. The time demands on each party may vary; one must reach an agreement before the other. If that is the case, then once a negotiator discovers that the time pressure on his adversary is greater than that on his side, he can stall the negotiations until the adversary must capitulate because of time. The tactics for stalling are many: plain delay, playing ill, being unable to attend meetings because of other meetings, and all sorts of other stalls that can make days turn into weeks and weeks turn into months, thereby placing greater and greater pressure on the adversary.

One young man used the stall to good advantage in gaining a pay raise from a niggardly employer. His superior wanted to know if the young man was going back to graduate school or not; the young man said that he hadn't made up his mind yet, and it would depend upon a lot of factors yet to be decided. Periodically the superior would nudge the young man for his decision, but each time he would be stalled. Finally, he made the offer, "If you will tell me today that you will stay for another year, I'll give you an additional $1000 a year raise. The subordinate accepted the offer. Admittedly, in a similar situation a superior could become angered and dismiss the man outright or demand a decision be made, but in this particular instance the subordinate had his superior sized up correctly and knew that he was under pressure as a replacement would be difficult to locate.

Sometimes stalls can cover a period of years in which the administrator simply hopes to outlive the adversary. Sometimes in legal battles a stall can be most advantageous. Witnesses can move away, memories can be dimmed, and all sorts of events can take place over a length of time that may strengthen one's hand in a legal conflict.

CAPITALIZE ON DEFEAT

Into the life of every administrator some rain must fall; he will lose on some issue. However, the adept loser capitalizes on defeat by extracting something from the winner as a consolation prize. Winners tend to be generous out of their natural psychological exhuberance over winning and are quite likely to grant some concessions if the loser takes his defeat gracefully.

A sales manager wanted to hire seven new men for better coverage of the marketing area, but he was flatly turned down by top management. However, in his defeat he was able to wring from management some much needed concessions for more liberalized expense accounts, something he had been trying to do for five years.

During one unfortunate year the dean of a large School of Business Administration lost a large number of his faculty to other schools. As it happened, each of these men left for various personal reasons, most of them did not improve themselves financially. However, the dean was able to use these resignations as a strong lever to gain some liberal salary increases for his remaining faculty. He presented the resignations to the administration, claiming that the men left for higher paying jobs.

The key to capitalizing on defeat is for the vanquished to control his behavior very carefully so that the winner will feel obligated to bestow some consolation. Should the administrator kick up a fuss over his defeat, it would be easy for the victor to rationalize his not giving any concessions.

Sometimes a truly astute administrator will offer a token battle in some matter he cares nothing about, not for the purpose of actually winning that battle but for what he can really get from it in defeat. It can be a psychologically advantageous position if one is owed some consolation prizes. However, this can be dangerous if overdone, for the administrator can look ridiculous if he automatically opposes any plan of action put forth.

WALTZ THEM TO THE COURTHOUSE STEPS

In some negotiations in which there are legal disputes, one must be prepared to take his adversaries right up to the courthouse steps and possibly into the courtroom if he is to get justice. Many foes simply refuse to negotiate realistically until they are brought into court, for they are well aware that the average person has a great aversion to going to court because of the costs, nuisance, and mental anguish involved in doing so. Consequently, many people will settle far short of their legitimate due just to stay out of court. People knowing this will seldom settle up until they are faced with the courtroom and the realities of all its ramifications. Hence the administrator in such cases should not dawdle around negotiating, but should file suit and take the adversary right up to the courthouse steps and negotiate from a stronger position.

On the other hand, when one is being sued by an adversary, he must be prepared to go right into court and not offer a settlement until both parties are on the courthouse steps, for the adversary is more likely to be willing to compromise advantageously at that time than earlier when he thinks he holds all the cards. A person who is afraid of going into court is at a distinct disadvantage in legal negotiations, and a great many negotiations come down to simply who is right or wrong legally.

Obviously, if one has a strong legal position his bargaining power is much greater than it would be otherwise, but one should not jump to the conclusion that a weak legal position robs him of all bargaining power. If the adversary has the strongest case imaginable, not having to go to court to collect it is of some value, and the only way you can get that value is by making him believe that he will have to go to court to get his just dues.

THE GRAPEVINE

Sometimes the wise administrator persuades his target indirectly by sending him messages informally via the grapevine. An office manager was distressed by the tardiness and overly long coffee breaks taken by his office staff. The situation had been degenerating for some time with people dragging in later and later and taking longer and longer coffee breaks. He hesitated to make an issue of the matter for fear of appearing to be a dictator. Nevertheless, he wanted to bring the practices under control. He asked his secretary to start the word along the grapevine that the people in the office should be more diligent about their work habits if they did not want them to be officially regulated.

The grapevine is a handy system to use when the administrator wants to pass down messages that are best not made in to formal orders. One of its advantages is that if it does not work, the formal order can come later with the administrator reaping little disadvantage from having first tried the grapevine.

THE VOTE

If the administrator is confident he has the majority of his people behind him on a plan, he can pretend to have a certain degree of neutrality and propose that a vote should be taken to decide what should be done on the matter. One of the advantages of being the boss is that one can choose when or when not to take a vote on an issue. The wise administrator does not take votes on matters where he knows he is going to be defeated. He will avoid at all costs votes on such issues for this lessens his prestige considerably.

There are certain dangers in submitting an issue to a vote, for there is always the chance that a meeting can run away from the administrator and, for one reason or another, the vote will not be acceptable to him, thereby posing a sticky problem.

The president of a conglomerate had been perplexed over what to do about a cable television system the company owned in a small town in the West. He and his vice president strongly wished to keep it in spite of its consistent cash losses and the fact that it had no hope for profitable operation in the future. Since some cable TV companies had made proposals to buy it, the president thought he would allow his board of directors to vote on the matter; he was confident that he could persuade the board to turn down the proposals. For the first time in the history of the firm, his board of directors overrode him and voted to sell. As an interesting sidelight, the president managed to cool the negotiations with the cable company as a stalling device in the hope that he could salvage the cable operation. At a board meeting one year later the board again instructed the president to sell off the subsidiary, which he was finally forced to do. Since that time the president has been very reluctant to submit anything to a vote of the board if he is in any way fearful of their decision. He only submits things that he has tested ahead of time with the individual directors so that he will not be surprised again.

FORCE THE ISSUE

Sometimes there is no persuading the other party for he is adamant in the matter; no amount of persuasion will change his opinion. In such cases administrators have been known to force the issue. A top-notch salesman whose territory was in Texas was quite unhappy over being discriminated against by the home office. While management furnished cars to its men, they were economy models devoid of such things as air conditioning. The salesman felt that air conditioning was an essential accessory in his territory and he had been trying to persuade his manager of his need for several years, without success. With the advent of the first 100° day of the year, the salesman sent a telegram to his manager that he was not going to work on any day that the temperature was over 90° until he was provided with an air conditioned car. This forced the issue: either give the man an air conditioned car, or fire him, or accept the layoff because of heat. The man won because he was an outstanding salesman and could not be replaced easily.

This tactic is obviously dangerous because most people strongly resent being forced to do anything against their will. It can only be used when the tactician is in a very strong position or he does not care about the consequences of losing on the tactic. Men frequently hand in their resignations to force an issue.

LISTEN

One of the soundest, least-used tactics in negotiation is careful, attentive listening; listening to the other person to detect exactly what it is that he wants and exactly where he stands. Careful listening frequently discloses a great many things. The adversary's tone, voice, and method of delivery frequently discloses his true motivation and feelings. Bluffs can be detected, lies discovered if one will but listen.

The nice thing about listening as a tactic is that it entails no dangers. It is completely safe to use and one gives away nothing to boot.

Listening is much broader than just paying attention to what people say to you. It also encompasses what they don't say, what they leave out. That discloses what they don't want you to know and chances are that is precisely what you do want to know.

Pay particular attention to just how the other person words his statements to you. Clever liars are able to deceive and not be brought to account for their deception upon discovery by technically telling the truth in the words actually spoken, but effectively communicating a lie by leading you to believe something else. A partner kept telling his associate that, "We have nothing to worry about!" in regard to a particular business deal that seemed to be in trouble. Well, when the roof caved in he was right —they had nothing to worry about. They had just lost their money, but it had been long gone and there had been nothing to worry about. Watch out for people who talk in generalities while you want specifics—they are evading the issue. Pin them down!

A great deal of money has been made, or saved, by a word overheard here or there. Go where the spirits flow, that's the garden where the indiscrete word grows.

A director of a small chemical company found himself sitting next to a thirsty sales manager of a competing company on a long cross-country flight. The director was also an investment counselor and had introduced himself as such. The sales manager spoke at great length about what he was doing, about company plans, about many valuable things. The director learned a great deal that afternoon that was converted into money shortly thereafter.

MAKE THEM THINK THEY'VE WON

The administrator is indeed clever who can win a victory, yet make the vanquished feel they have won. This is not as difficult as it might seem, for many times the two parties are fighting for different goals. Even in negotiations, where the administrator has the best of the compromise, he might profitably make the vanquished feel he has the best of the bargain. This tactic can work because many times the other party does not know the real basis against which to compare a relative victory or loss. A union leader may feel that he won a victory in getting a 15¢ per hour raise for his workers and the employer can let him feel that way, but the employer may feel that he has won the victory because he thought he was going to have to pay 25¢ and was prepared to do so. Automobile dealers are past masters at this game, by always trying to make a customer feel that they got a bargain price on their new car.

There are few dangers in using this tactic, because everyone likes to believe he is a winner, whether or not down deep he really is convinced of this or not. It is most important that at least he is able to have the appearance of being a victor.

AVOID PERSONALITIES

Avoid, at all costs, dealing in personalities. Instead, focus your arguments around the facts of a case. Never call the adversary names or attack him personally or question his honesty or sincerity even though you may be severely provoked to do so. Such attacks only arouse emotional antagonisms. No matter how unscrupulous or questionable the adversary's tactics may be, it is probably advisable to avoid comment directly about his personality.

A disappointed subordinate confronted his boss in the office one day to ask for a raise. When his overtures were spurned, he accused the superior of breaking his word and made statements blaming him personally for lack of advancement. This was a serious blunder, no matter how true it might have been, because no one likes to be called a liar. Wise men seek to blame other forces outside the executive's control. He might reply to the superior, "I realize that you would like to give me this additional money if you could, but that the conditions of this company are such that it is not possible at this time. Could you tell me exactly what it is that is holding up my advancement and when I might expect it?" Personal attacks usually sever communications and can permanently alienate the parties to such a degree that relations becomes impossible.

PLANT THE SEED

In dealing with some types of people, the administrator must be quite unobtrusive in seeming to persuade them to do something. In such circumstances he is able, many times, to reach his desired ends by merely planting a certain seed in the mind of the right party. Suggestion is a potent persuasive tactic. Sometimes an entire plan can be suggested by merely planting a seed of thought in the mind of the right individual.

The president of a large electronics company wanted to discontinue a huge Christmas party that the company had given annually to its employees because the affair had become unmanageable. One year in October, because of depressed conditions in the industry, the company had to lay off a large number of production workers. In a "chance" meeting with the shop steward, the president casually voiced concern over the plight of the people laid off, with Christmas coming up and all. In an apparent off-hand manner, he commented that he felt rather guilty about the company spending money on the Christmas party with all of the laid off people having a hard time of it. He casually said, "It's too bad we can't give them the money instead of drinking it up." The seed was planted and it grew. Within the week there was a formal request by the union that the money the company normally spent on the Christmas party be divided among the people laid off. The president commended the union on coming up with such a noble idea.

This is an exceedingly sound tactic to use as frequently as possible, for it achieves maximum persuasive impact as the adversary thinks it was his idea, and when he proposes it you make him look good by complimenting him on his wisdom and judgment. There is little to be lost by trying this tactic, for if it doesn't work something else can be tried later. The major disadvantage of it is that it may take time to execute and the precise plan the other person may come up with might not exactly be what the administrator had in mind.

WHERE THE BODY'S BURIED—BLACKMAIL

It has not been unknown for administrators to use blackmail to achieve their goals and the foundations of this tactic rest in knowing where the adversary has buried his bodies. Of course, this can be an exceedingly dangerous tactic to use, unless one is quite certain of his facts and the hold they will have over an adversary, for few people approve of blackmail. The most effective use of this tactic is in just knowing where the bodies are buried, but not overtly using them for blackmail purposes. The secretary who knows the peculiar behavior deviations of her boss need not bring up the matter to him in order for her to achieve some of her goals.

Conversely, the wise administrator makes certain that his adversaries never learn where his bodies are buried, lest they be used against him at the most inopportune time. One executive made the mistake of allowing his secretary to learn of certain freedoms he was taking with his expense account. The day came when she used this knowledge to protect her job to the embarrassment of the administrator. Another man, during an hour of relaxation at a local watering hole with a peer, disclosed that he had been fired from his last job for suspicion of treating corporate finances as his own. This information found its way into the wrong ears to the good of no one.